THE KING JAMES BIBLE

WHY HAVE MODERN BIBLE
TRANSLATIONS REMOVED MANY VERSES
THAT ARE IN THE KING JAMES VERSION?

Edward D. Andrews

THE KING JAMES BIBLE

Why Have Modern Bible Translations Removed Many Verses That Are In the King James Version?

The Truth Shall Set You Free

Edward D. Andrews

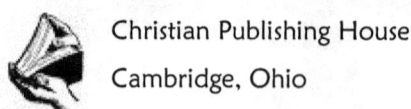

Christian Publishing House
Cambridge, Ohio

CHRISTIAN PUBLISHING HOUSE
CONSERVATIVE CHRISTIAN BOOKS
APOLOGETIC DEFENSE OF GOD, THE
FAITH, THE BIBLE, AND CHRISTIANITY

Copyright © 2019 Christian Publishing House

All rights reserved. Except for brief quotations in articles, other publications, book reviews, and blogs, no part of this book may be reproduced in any manner without prior written permission from the publishers. For information, write, support@christianpublishers.org

Unless otherwise stated, Scripture quotations are from the Updated American Standard Version (UASV) Copyright © 2018 by Christian Publishing House

THE KING JAMES BIBLE: Why Have Modern Bible Translations Removed Many Verses That Are In the King James Version?

Authored by Edward D Andrews

ISBN-13: **978-1-949586-96-1**

ISBN-10: **1-949586-96-0**

TRANSLATIONS Referred to in this Publication vii
INTRODUCTION 9
    Glossary of Technical Terms 11
CHAPTER 1 Dutch Bible and Textual Scholar Erasmus of Rotterdam 15
    Erasmus' Early Life 16
    The First Greek Text 17
    Erasmus Contrasted with Luther 18
    The Textus Receptus 20
CHAPTER 2 How the King James Version Became Popular 23
    Bible Translation Increases Momentum 23
    Overcoming the Difficulties 24
    A Literary Masterpiece 25
    Acts 1:8 "To the Uttermost Part of the Earth" 26
    The Need for Change 27
    A Valuable Modern Translation 29
CHAPTER 3 Why Have Modern Bible Translations Removed Verses That Are In The King James Version 30
    Taking Liberties with the Text 30
CHAPTER 4 The Trustworthiness of Early Copyists 34
    Returning to the First Century 42
    Blinded by Misguided Perceptions 44
    The New Testament Compared to Classical Literature 45
    Were the Scribes in the Early Centuries Amateurs? 46
CHAPTER 5 Manuscripts Separated Into Families Down to The Printed Text of the Greek New Testament 55
    Separated Into Families 55
    The Corruption Period 56
    Desiderius Erasmus and the Greek Text 57

Erasmus' Early Life 58
The First Greek Text 59
Erasmus Contrasted With Luther 60
The Textus Receptus 62
The Restoration Period 64
The Climax of the Restored Text 65

CHAPTER 6 Modern Bible Translations Have Been Accused of Removing Words, Phrases, Sentences, Who Verses, Even Whole Sections 67

The Warning 67
Copying Manuscripts 68
Scribes Taking Liberties 69
The Restoration Period Reiterated for Emphasis 73
The Climax of the Restored Text 75
Some Verses That Should Not Have Ever Been 76
Trusting the Greek New Testament 86

CHAPTER 7 Do You Really Know the King James Version? 87

Early English Bible History 89
The Irony of It All 90
Changes to the King James Version 92
The Sixteen Missing Verses Or The Sixteen Added Verses? 94

CHAPTER 8 KING JAMES VERSION Read the Bible to Understand It .. 105

Above All Acquire Wisdom 105
Language Changes Obscure Understanding 107

CHAPTER 9 The Arrival of the Critical Text Behind Our Modern-Day Bible Translations 114

The Fifteen Rules of Griesbach 115
Critical Rules of Westcott & Hort 123
Setting Straight the Indefensible Defenders of the Textus Receptus 124

CHAPTER 10 The Reign of the King James Version Is Over.................. 131
    What is the Mystery of Godliness? 137
    Scribal Interpolations 138
    Both a Science and an Art 140
    Why We Can Have Confidence?..142

CHAPTER 11 Why Do We Not Need the Original Bible Manuscripts?...143
    Manuscripts Saved from Egyptian Garbage Heaps......................145

CHAPTER 12 CPH Principles of Bible Translation for the Updated American Standard Version...148
    UPDATED AMERICAN STANDARD VERSION (UASV) 156

CHAPTER 13 The Updated American Standard Version (UASV) 158
    Why UASV? 158
    Updated American Standard Version's Story 159
    Trials and Tribulations 159

OTHER BOOKS BY EDWARD D. ANDREWS 161

Bibliography..163

TRANSLATIONS Referred to in this Publication

Unless otherwise indicated, Scripture quotations are from the *Updated American Standard Version of the Holy Scriptures*, 2016 (UASV). Abbreviations used to designate other translations of the Bible are provided below:

- **ASV:** American Standard Version (1901)
- **AMP:** Amplified Bible (1987)
- **AT:** The Bible – An American Translation (1935)
- **CEB:** Common English Bible (2011)
- **CEV:** Contemporary English Version (1995)
- **DARBY:** Darby Translation (1890)
- **ERV:** Easy to Read Version (2012)
- **GW:** GOD'S WORD Translation (1995)
- **GNT:** Good News Translation (1992)
- **HCSB:** Holman Christian Standard Bible (2003)
- **JB:** The Jerusalem Bible (1966)
- **JP:** The Holy Scriptures According to the Masoretic Text (1917)
- **KJV:** King James Version (1611, 1942)
- **LEB:** Lexham English Bible (LEB)
- **LXX:** Greek Septuagint Version of Hebrew Old Testament (280-150 B.C.E.)
- **NCV:** New Century Version (2005)
- **NEB:** New English Bible (1970)
- **NLV:** New Life Version (1969)
- **NLT:** New Living Translation (2013)

- **NTB:** A New Translation of the Bible (1934)
- **NASB:** New American Standard Bible (1995)

NET: New English Translation (2006) Biblical Studies Press

NIV: New International Version (2011)

NIVI: New International Version Inclusive Language Edition (1996)

NKJV: New King James Version (1982)

NLT: New Living Translation (2007)

NLV: New Language Version (1969)

NRSV: New Revised Standard Version (1989)

PHILIPS: New Testament in Modern English (1958)

REB: Revised English Bible (1989)

RSV: Revised Standard Version (1971)

SEB: Simple English Bible (1980)

TEB: The Emphasised Bible (1897)

TEV: Today's English Version (1976)

TLB: The Living Bible (1971)

TNIV: Today's New International Version (2005)

UASV: Updated American Standard Version (2013-18 Work in progress)[1]

WHNU: Westcott-Hort Greek New Testament / Nestle-Aland Greek New Testament, United Bible Society Greek New Testament (1881, 2012, 1993)

YLT: Young's Literal Translation (1887)

---

[1] The UASV is projected to be completed by 2019. However, we are using verses herein of the books that are completed at present.

INTRODUCTION

What is Bible translation? In short, it is the rendering of something written or spoken in one language in words of a different language. However, there are two basic philosophies or methods on how this is to be accomplished. There is the **literal translation**, i.e., lexical or linguistic translation, whose translator or translation committee is determining what English word or phrase in the Hebrew-English or Greek-English lexicon (the technical term for dictionary) corresponds best to the original language word. For example, the Greek word *phronema* can be translated differently as the corresponding English terms are "mind" or "mindset." Therefore, the American Standard Version (ASV), English Standard Version (ESV), and New American Standard Bible (NASB) render *phronema* in Romans 8:27 as "he who searches hearts knows what is the **mind** of the Spirit." However, the Lexham English Bible (LEB) and the Holman Christian Standard Bible (HCSB) render *phronema* as "the one who searches our hearts knows what the **mindset** of the Spirit is" and "He who searches the hearts knows the Spirit's mindset" respectively. Both of these renderings are literal.

The literal translation committee is focused on the original language term, with the goal of determining which English word(s) in the lexicon correspond best. The other translation method is known as the **dynamic or functional equivalent** method (Defined below). Their committee is interested in the reader, and the end goal is to take the corresponding English term and find the sense of what is meant, which replaces the literal rendering. Therefore, the Common English Bible (CEB) and the New Life Version (NLV) render *phronema* in Romans 8:27 as "knows how the Spirit **thinks**,"[2] while the Easy to Read Version (ERV) and the New Living Translation (NLT) render it, "understands what the Spirit is **saying**." Below is phronema in Romans 8:6-7 in three literal translations, followed by three dynamic equivalents. The sense of phronema is "what one has in the mind, the thought" (the content of the process expressed in phroneo, "to have in mind, to think"); or "an object of thought" (Vine 1996, Volume 2, Page 409) Logos Bible Software has "**mindset** n. – a habitual or characteristic mental attitude that determines how you will interpret and respond to situations." (Bible Sense Lexicon)

---

[2] It should be admitted that "thinking" is actually a literal rendering of *phronema*, but the more literal of the three would be "mind" and "mindset."

Romans 8:6-7 English Standard Version (ESV)	Romans 8:6-7 New American Standard Bible (NASB)	Romans 8:6-7 Updated American Standard Version (UASV)
⁶ For to set the **mind** on the flesh is death, but to set the **mind** on the Spirit is life and peace. ⁷ For the **mind** that is set on the flesh is hostile to God, for it does not submit to God's law; indeed, it cannot.	⁶ For the **mind set** on the flesh is death, but the **mind set** on the Spirit is life and peace, ⁷ because the **mind set** on the flesh is hostile toward God; for it does not subject itself to the law of God, for it is not even able *to do so*,	⁶ For setting the **mind** on the flesh is death, but setting the mind on the spirit is life and peace ⁷ because setting the **mind** on the flesh means enmity toward God, for it is not subjected to the law of God, for it is not even able to do so
Romans 8:6-7 Common English Bible (CEB)	Romans 8:6-7 Easy-to-Read Version (ERV)	Romans 8:6-7 New Century Version (NCV)
⁶ The **attitude** that comes from selfishness leads to death, but the **attitude** that comes from the Spirit leads to life and peace. ⁷ So the **attitude** that comes from selfishness is hostile to God. It doesn't submit to God's Law, because it can't.	⁶ If your **thinking** is controlled by your sinful self, there is spiritual death. But if your **thinking** is controlled by the Spirit, there is life and peace. ⁷ Why is this true? Because anyone whose **thinking** is controlled by their sinful self is against God. They refuse to obey God's law. And really they are not able to obey it.	⁶ If people's **thinking** is controlled by the sinful self, there is death. But if their **thinking** is controlled by the Spirit, there is life and peace. ⁷ When people's **thinking** is controlled by the sinful self, they are against God, because they refuse to obey God's law and really are not even able to obey God's law.

Glossary of Technical Terms

Time is in one direction and cannot be repeated. B.C.E. means "before the Common Era," which is more accurate than B.C. ("before Christ"). C.E. denotes "Common Era," often called A.D., for *anno Domini*, meaning "in the year of our Lord." It should be noted that the Romans did not have a zero, so time goes from 1 B.C.E. to 1 C.E.

4026   1000   760   406   ◀B.C.E. | C.E.▶   29   33   36   100

Original Language (OL) is the Hebrew and Aramaic for the Old Testament and Greek for the New Testament.

Source Language (SL) is the language in which a translation is being produced in another. Therefore, if one is translating from Hebrew into English, then Hebrew is the SL.

Receptor Language (RL) is just the opposite; it is the language in which the translation is being produced. Therefore, if one is translating from Greek into English, then English is the RL.

As you can see from the above, the terms **S**ource and **R**eceptor Language have the acronym SL and RL respectively. In addition, keep in mind that the text that the translator is rendering into another language is the source text. Please do not confuse the Source Language with the Original Language. True, the Source Language can be the Original Language of say Hebrew or Greek. However, if there is a case of a translator making a Chinese translation of the New Testament, but has chosen to make it from English, the Source Language would be English. The Original language of the Old Testament is Hebrew, and the New Testament is Greek.

Dynamic Equivalent (DE) is taking the meaning of the original language text in the receptor language of say English and focusing on the sense of the word. For example, at Exodus 35:21, the English Standard Version (ESV) literally reads "And they came, everyone whose **heart** stirred him," while the Common English Bible (CEB) committee deemed the figurative use of the "heart" as too difficult, so they rendered it, "Everyone who was excited and eager." The objective of the dynamic equivalent is to translate meaning not words.

Dynamic Equivalence is a method of translation, which is also known as a *sense-for-sense* or *thought-for-thought* translation, whose objective is to translate the meaning of phrases or whole sentences. The objective is to take technical terms, idiomatic expressions, figurative language, and so on, and render them in easy to understand terms that they feel reflect the sense of the OL terms.

Functional Equivalence (FE) is a method of translation that goes beyond the corresponding English word or phrase of the original language, with what is known as a functional equivalent. Again, when the literal rendering is determined to be too difficult for the modern-day reader, the committee will like for a word or phrase that they feel captures the sense of what was meant. For example, the literal NASB at Proverbs 4:15, reads "Drink water from your own cistern," while the functional equivalents ERV reads, "Now, about sex and marriage," and the NCV reads, "Be faithful to your own wife." The FE is attempting to explain the imagery that is found in the literal Translation.

Formal Equivalence (FE) is a word-for-word translation, where the committee gives the reader the corresponding English word, attempting to follow the same word order as the OL. The emphasis is on the OL and the lexical or linguistic interpretation, as well as the grammatical construction.

Literal Translation (LT) gives you what God said, so there is no concealing this by going beyond into the realms of what a translator interprets the sense of these words.

Target Audience (TA) is the audience that the publisher is focusing on reaching with their translation. Once that target audience has been chosen; then, the committee will have this translation philosophy mindset. For example, the Common English Bible target audience is a seventh-grade reading level, "to make the Bible accessible to a broad range of people; it's written at a comfortable level for over half of all English readers."[3]

Portions of scripture were assigned to each of the 120 translators. Each produced a draft translation which was then reviewed and modified by a co-translator. The resulting text was then sent to one of 77 "reading groups," teams of five to ten non-specialists that read it out loud and noted awkward translations. The rendering, along with suggestions for improvement, was then sent to a readability editor to check style and grammar, followed by a complete review by the editor for that section of the Bible. The text was then put before the entire editorial board which resolved any lingering controversies and ensured consistency throughout the entire Bible translation.[4]

---

[3] http://www.commonenglishbible.com/
[4] http://en.wikipedia.org/wiki/Common_English_Bible

Mark 6:12 Updated American Standard Version (UASV)	Mark 6:12 Common English Bible (CEB)
¹² And they went out and proclaimed that men⁵ should repent.	¹² So they went out and proclaimed that people should change their hearts and lives.
Romans 12:2 Updated American Standard Version (UASV)	**Romans 12:2** Common English Bible (CEB)
² And do not be conformed to this world, but be transformed by the renewing of your mind, so that you may prove what the will of God is, that which is good and acceptable⁶ and perfect.	Don't be conformed to the patterns of this world, but be transformed by the renewing of your minds so that you can figure out what God's will is--what is good and pleasing and mature.

The Search for the Best Translation

It is a daunting task for the new Bible student to walk into a Christian bookstore to purchase a Bible. Immediately, he is met with shelves upon shelves of more than 100 different English translation choices: NIV, TNIV, ESV, NASB, UASV, NRSV, CEV, HCSB, NLT, KJV, and on and on. He is even further bewildered when he realizes that there are different formats within each translation: a standard format, a reference Bible, a study Bible, a life application Bible, an archaeology Bible, to name just a few. He further notices that some translations claim to be literal (word-for-word) while others claim to be dynamic or functional equivalent (thought for thought), which has only served to increase his confusion.

God has chosen to convey an extremely important message to the human family, one that is a matter of life and death. In the Bible of 66 smaller books, we find God's will and purpose for us, as well as what role we need to play, in order to receive the gift of life. Sir Matthew Hale, Lord Chief Justice of England, once said, "The Bible is the only source of all Christian truth; the only rule for the Christian life; the only book that unfolds to us the realities of eternity." (Edwards 1908, p. 40)

If we are to know God, it only makes sense that we must know his Word, the Bible. Jesus Christ makes this all too clear to us when he said in

---

⁵ I.e., means both men and women
⁶ Or *well-pleasing*

prayer to his Father: "This is eternal life: that they may know You, the only true God, and the One You have sent, Jesus Christ." (John 17:3, HCSB) Here we see that "eternal life" is closely related to our knowing (having a relationship with) God and his Son, Jesus Christ. It is the apostle John who answers the why: "And the world with its lust is passing away, but the one who does God's will remain forever." 1 John 2:17, ESV.

In order to know "the will of God," we must recognize that the Bible is our only guide in this matter. Each Christian should "be filled with the knowledge [lit., accurate or full knowledge] of his will in all spiritual wisdom and understanding, to walk worthily of the Lord unto all pleasing, bearing fruit in every good work, and increasing in the knowledge [lit., accurate or full knowledge] of God." (Col. 1:9, 10, NASB) Is it possible to "walk worthily" of God without fully knowing his will? Is it possible to know his will without first understanding the Bible?

Psalm 119:165 Updated American Standard Version (UASV)

[165] Abundant peace belongs to those loving your law,
And for them, there is no stumbling-block.

At times, it must be difficult for us to contemplate the idea of finding any measure of peace in the world we now know. It is our love for God's law and the application of that law, which will give us a righteous standing before our Creator (being justified in his eyes) and a measure of peace and happiness now. Thus, the incentive to know our Bible is far greater than one might have thought, meaning we are seeking approval in God's eyes as well as peace and happiness and the hope of a future everlasting life.

Looking Behind the Curtain

Have you ever wondered how the actual translation process works? Why is the same Hebrew Old Testament or Greek New Testament word translated differently in the same translation, and even interpreted in others? Christians, who have never worked in the field of translation, have long thought that words are codes. In other words, the translator has the Hebrew or Greek text on one side, to which he simply plugs in an English word for each Greek word, resulting in the English translation. What we will discover in CGBT is that far more is involved in the translation process. However, we will also discover that one translation method goes beyond the Word of God, becoming, in essence, an interpretive translation. Before delving into the issues at hand, chapter 1 will introduce to Desiderius Erasmus, the Bible scholar behind the master Greek text (aka critical text) that would bring on the controversy within translations centuries later.

CHAPTER 1 Dutch Bible and Textual Scholar Erasmus of Rotterdam

I WOULD have these words translated into all languages, so that not only Scots and Irish, but Turks and Saracens too might read them . . . I long for the ploughboy to sing them to himself as he follows his plough, the weaver to hum them to the tune of his shuttle, the traveler to beguile with them the dullness of his journey. (Clayton 2006, 230)

Dutch scholar Desiderius Erasmus penned those words in the early part of the 16th century. Like his English counterpart, William Tyndale, it was his greatest desire that God's Word is widely translated and that even the plowboy would have access to it.

Much time has passed since the Reformation, and 98 percent of the world we live in today has access to the Bible. There is little wonder that the Bible has become the bestseller of all time. It has influenced men from all walks of life to fight for freedom and truth. This is especially true during the Reformation of Europe throughout the 16th century. These leading men were of great faith, courage, and strength, such as Martin Luther, William Tyndale, while others, like Erasmus, was more subtle in the change that he produced. Thus, it has been said of the Reformation that Martin Luther only opened the door to it after Erasmus picked the lock.

There is not one historian of the period, who would deny that Erasmus was a great scholar. Remarking on his character, the *Catholic Encyclopedia* says: "He had an unequaled talent for form, great journalistic gifts, a surpassing power of expression: for strong and moving discourse, keen irony, and covert sarcasm, he was unsurpassed." (Vol. 5, p. 514) Consequently, when Erasmus went to see Sir Thomas More, the Lord Chancellor of England, just before Erasmus made himself known, More was so impressed with his exchange that he shortly said: "You are either Erasmus or the Devil."

The wit of Erasmus was evidenced in a response that he gave to Frederick, elector of Saxony, who asked him what he thought about Martin Luther. Erasmus retorted, "Luther has committed two blunders; he has ventured to touch the crown of the pope and the bellies of the monks." (*Cyclopedia of Biblical, Theological, and Ecclesiastical Literature*: Vol. 3 – p, 279) However, we must ask what type of influence did the Bible have on Erasmus and, in turn, what did he do to affect its future? First, let us look at the early years of Erasmus' life.

Erasmus' Early Life

He was born in Rotterdam, the Netherlands, in 1466. He was not a happy boy living in a home as the illegitimate son of a Dutch priest. He was faced with the double tragedy of his mother's death at seventeen, and his father shortly thereafter. His guardians ignored his desire to enter the university; rather they sent him to the Augustinian monastery of Steyn. Erasmus gained a vast knowledge of the Latin language, the classic as well as the Church Fathers. In time, this type of life was so detestable to him; he jumped on the opportunity, at the age of twenty-six, to become secretary to the bishop of Cambrai, Henry of Bergen, in France. This afforded him his chance to enter university studies in Paris. However, he was a sickly man, always ill, suffering from poor health throughout his entire life.

It was in 1499 that Erasmus was invited to visit England. It was here that he met Thomas More, John Colet and other theologians in London, which fortified his resolution to apply himself to Biblical studies. In order to understand the Bible's message better, he applied himself more fully in his study of Greek, soon being able to teach it to others. It was around this time that Erasmus penned a treatise entitled Handbook of the Christian Soldier, in which he advised the young Christian to study the Bible, saying: "There is nothing that you can believe with greater certitude than what you read in these writings." (Erasmus and Dolan 1983, 37)

While trying to escape the plague, make a living in an economy that had bottomed worse than our 20th century Great Depression, Erasmus found himself at Louvain, Belgium, in 1504. It was here that he fell in love with the study of textual criticism while visiting the Monastery of Parc. Within the library, Erasmus discovered a manuscript of Italian scholar Lorenzo Valla: *Annotations on the New Testament*. Textual criticism is an art and science that studies manuscripts, evaluating internal and external evidence, especially of the Bible or works of literature, in order to determine which readings are the original or most authentic. Erasmus had commissioned himself toward the task of restoring the original text of the Greek New Testament.

Erasmus moved on to Italy and subsequently pushed on to England once again. It is this trip that brought to mind his original meeting with Thomas More, meditating on the origin of More's name (*moros*, Greek for "a fool"); he penned a write or satire, which he called Praise of Folly. In this work, Erasmus takes the abstract quality "folly" as being a human being and pictured it as encroaching in all aspects of life, but nowhere is folly more in obvious than amid the theologians and clergy. This is his subtle way of exposing the abuses of the clergy. It is these abuses, which had brought on the Reformation that was now festering. "As to the popes," he wrote, "if they claim to be the successors of the Apostles, they should consider that the same things are required of them as were practiced by their predecessors." Instead of doing this, he perceived, they believe that "to teach the people is too laborious; to interpret the scripture is to invade the prerogative of the schoolmen; to pray is too idle." There is little wonder that it was said of Erasmus that he had "a surpassing power of expression"! (Nichols 2006, Vol. 2, 6)

The First Greek Text

Whilst teaching Greek at Cambridge University in England, Erasmus continued with his work of revising the text of the Greek New Testament. One of his friends, Martin Dorpius, attempted to persuade him that the Latin did not need to be corrected from the Greek. Dorpius makes the same error in thinking that the "King James Only" people make, arguing: "For is it likely that the whole Catholic Church would have erred for so many centuries, seeing that she has always used and sanctioned this translation? Is it probable that so many holy fathers, so many consummate scholars would have longed to convey a warning to a friend?" (Campbell 1949, 71) Thomas More joined Erasmus in replying to these arguments, making the point that the importance lies within having an accurate text in the original languages.

In Basel, Switzerland, Erasmus was about to be hassled by the printer Johannes Froben. Froben was alerted that Cardinal Ximenes of Toledo, Spain, had been putting together a Greek and Latin Testament in 1514. However, he was delaying publication until he had the whole Bible completed. The first printed Greek critical text would have set the standard, with the other being all but ignored. Erasmus published his first edition in 1516, while the Complutensian Polyglot (many languages) was not issued until 1522

The fact that Erasmus was rushed to no end resulted in a Greek text that contained hundreds of typographical errors alone.[1] Textual scholar Scrivener once stated: '[It] is in that respect the most faulty book I know,' (Scrivener 1894, 185) This comment does not even take into consideration the blatant interpolations (insert readings) into the text that were not part of the original. Erasmus was not lost to the typographical errors, which corrected a good many in later editions. This did not include the textual errors. It was his second edition of 1519 that was used by Martin Luther in his German translation and William Tyndale's English translation. This is exactly what Erasmus wanted, writing the following in that edition's preface: "I would have these words translated into all languages. . . . I long for the ploughboy to sing them to himself as he follows his plough."

Sadly, the continuous reproduction of this debased Greek New Testament, gave rise to it becoming the standard, being called the Textus Receptus (Received Text), taking over 400 years before it was dethroned by the critical Text of B. F. Westcott and F. J. A. Hort in 1881. Regardless of its imperfection, the Erasmus critical edition began the all-important work of textual criticism, which has only brought about a better critical text, as well as more accurate Bible translations.

As was true with many other early Bibles in the early days of the Reformation, it had its detractors. Like the Geneva Bible, but on a much tamer note, Erasmus was critical of the clergy in his notes. For instance, the text of Matthew 16:18, which says, "Thou art Peter, and upon this rock I will build my church." (Douay) Very plainly, he rejects the idea that this text is applied to primacy Peter, and that the pope is a successor of such. Imagine writing such a thing in the very edition you are going to dedicate to the pope! We can certainly see why Erasmus' works were prohibited, even in the universities.

Erasmus was not only concerned with ascertaining the original words; he was just as concerned with achieving an accurate understanding of those words. In 1519, he penned Principles of True Theology (shortened to The Ratio). Herein he introduces his principles for Bible study, his interpretation rules. Among them is the thought of never taking a quotation out of its context nor out of the line of thought of its author. Erasmus saw the Bible as a whole work by one author, and it should interpret itself.

Erasmus Contrasted with Luther

Erasmus penned a treatise called Familiar Colloquies in 1518, where again he was exposing the corruptions on the Church and the monasteries. Just one year earlier, in 1517, Martin Luther had nailed his 95 theses on the church door at Wittenberg, denouncing the indulgences, the scandal that had rocked numerous countries. Many folks were likely thinking that these two could bring change and reform. This was not going to be a team effort, though, as they both were at opposite ends of the spectrum on how to bring this reform about. Luther would come to condemn Erasmus, because he was viewed as being too moderate, seeking to make change peacefully within the Church. Many have viewed it as Erasmus thinking and writing, while Luther appeared to go beyond that with his actions.

The seemingly small bond they may have shared (by way of their writings against the Church establishment), was torn down the middle in 1524 when Erasmus penned the essay On the Freedom of the Will. Luther believed that salvation results from "justification by faith alone" (Latin, sola fide) and not from priestly absolution or works of penance. In fact, Luther was so adamant on his belief of "justification by faith alone" that in his Bible translation, he added the word "alone" to Romans 3:28. What Luther failed to understand was that Paul was writing about the works of the Mosaic Law. (Romans 3:19, 20, 28) Thus, Luther denied the notion that man possesses a free will. However, Erasmus would not accept such faulty reasoning, in that it would make God unjust because this would suggest that man would be unable to act in such a way as to affect his salvation.

As the Reformation was growing throughout Europe, Erasmus saw complaints from both sides. Many of the religious leaders who supported the reform movement chose to leave the Catholic Church. While they could not predict the result of their decision, they moved forward, many ending in death. This would not be true of Erasmus though, for he withdrew from the debate, yet he did refuse to be made cardinal. His approach was to try to appease both sides. Thus, Rome saw his writings as being that of a heretic, prohibiting them, while the reformers denounced him as refusing to risk his life for the cause. Here was a man, emotionally broken over criticism, but in fear of rocking the boat with Rome, so he cautiously sat on the sideline.

The affairs of Erasmus to the Reformation can be summarized as follows: "He was a reformer until the Reformation became a fearful reality; a jester at the bulwarks of the papacy until they began to give way; a propagator of the Scriptures until men betook themselves to the study and the application of them; depreciating the mere outward forms of religion until they had come to be estimated at their real value; in short, a learned, ingenious, benevolent, amiable, timid, irresolute man, who, bearing the responsibility, resigned to others the glory of rescuing the human mind from the bondage of a thousand years. The distance between his career and that of Luther was therefore continually enlarging, until they at length moved in opposite directions, and met each other with mutual animosity."— (McClintock and Strong 1894, 278).

The greatest gain from the Reformation is that the common person can now hold God's Word in his hand. In fact, the Englishperson has over 100 different translations from which to choose. From these 16th-century life and death struggles, in which Erasmus shared, there has materialized dependable and accurate Bible translations. Consequently, the 'plowboy' of 98 percent of the world can pick up his Bible, or at least part of it.

The Textus Receptus

The Dark Ages (5th to 15th centuries C.E.), was a time when the Church had the Bible locked up in the Latin language, and scholarship and learning were nearly nonexistent. However, with the birth of the Morning Star of the Reformation, John Wycliffe (1328-1384), and more officially in the 16th century Reformation, and the invention of the printing press in 1455, the restraints were loosened, and there was a rebirth of interest in the Greek language. Moreover, with the fall of Constantinople to the Turks 1453 C. E., many Greek scholars and their manuscripts were scattered abroad, resulting in a revival of Greek in the Western citadels of learning.

About fifty years later, or at the beginning of the sixteenth century, Ximenes, archbishop of Toledo, Spain, a man of rare capability and honor, invited foremost scholars of his land to his university at Alcala to produce a multiple-language Bible, not for the common people, but for the educated. The outcome would be the Polyglot, named Complutensian corresponding to the Latin of Alcala. This would be a Bible of six large volumes, beautifully bound, containing the Old Testament in four languages (Hebrew, Aramaic, Greek, and Latin) and the New Testament in two (Greek and Latin). For the Greek New Testament, these scholars had only a few manuscripts available to them, and those of late origin. One may wonder why this was the case when they were supposed to have access to the Vatican library. This Bible was completed in 1514, providing the first printed Greek New Testament, but did not receive approval by the pope to be published until 1520 and was not released to the public until 1522.

Froben, a printer in Basel, Switzerland became aware of the completion of the Complutensian Polyglot Bible and of its pending consent by the pope to be published. Immediately, he saw a prospect of making profits. He at once sent word to the Dutch scholar Desiderius Erasmus (1469-1536), who was the foremost European scholar of the day and whose works he had published in Latin, beseeching him to hurry through a Greek New Testament text. In an attempt to bring the first published Greek text to completion, Erasmus was only able to locate, in July of 1515, a few late cursive manuscripts for collating and preparing his text. It would go to press in October of 1515 and would be completed by March of 1516. In fact, Erasmus was in such a hurried mode he rushed the manuscript containing the Gospels to the printer without first editing it, making such changes, as he felt was necessary on the proof sheets. Because of this great rush job, this work also contained hundreds of typographical errors. Erasmus himself admitted this in its preface that it was "rushed through rather than edited."

Bruce Metzger referred to the Erasmian text as a "debased form of the Greek Testament." (B. M. Metzger 1964, 1968, 1992, 103)

Needless to say, Erasmus was moved to produce an improved text in four succeeding editions of 1519, 1522, 1527, and 1535. Erasmus' editions of the Greek text, we are informed, ended up being an excellent achievement, a literary sensation. They were inexpensive, and the first two editions totaled 3,300 copies, in comparison to the 600 copies of the large and expensive six-volume Polyglot Bible. In the preface to his first edition, Erasmus stated, "I vehemently dissent from those who would not have private persons read the Holy Scriptures, nor have them translated into the vulgar tongues." (Baer 2007, 268)

Except for everyday practical consideration, the editions of Erasmus had little to vouch for them, for he had access to five (some say eight) Greek manuscripts of reasonably late origin and none of these were of the whole Greek New Testament. Rather, these comprised one or more sections into which the Greek texts were normally divided: (1) the Gospels; (2) Acts and the general epistles (James through Jude); (3) the letters of Paul; (4) Revelation. In fact, of the 5,800 Greek New Testament manuscripts that we now have, only about fifty are complete.

Consequently, Erasmus had but one copy of Revelation (twelfth century). Since it was incomplete, he merely retranslated the missing last six verses of the book from the Latin Vulgate back into Greek. He even frequently brought his Greek text in line with the Latin Vulgate; this is why there are some twenty readings in his Greek text not found in any other Greek manuscript.

Martin Luther would use Erasmus' 1519 edition for his German translation, and William Tyndale would use the 1522 edition for his English translation. Erasmus' editions were also the foundation for further Greek editions of the New Testament by others. For instance, the four published by Robert Estienne (Stephanus, 1503-59). According to Bruce Metzger, the third of these, published by Stephanus, in 1550, became the Textus Receptus or Received Text of Britain and the basis of the King James Version. This took place through Theodore de Beza (1519-1605), whose work was based on the corrupted third and fourth editions of the Erasmian text. Beza would produce nine editions of the Greek text, four being independent (1565, 1589, 1588-9, 1598), and the other five smaller reprints. It would be two of Beza's editions, that of 1589 and 1598, which would become the English Received Text.

Beza's Greek edition of the New Testament did not even differ as much as might be expected from those of Erasmus. Why do I say, as might be expected? Beza was a friend of the Protestant reformer, John Calvin, succeeding him at Geneva, and was also a well-known classical and biblical scholar. In addition, Beza possessed two important Greek manuscripts of the fourth and fifth century, the **D** and **D**ᵖ (also known as **D²**), the former of which contains most of the Gospels and Acts, as well as a fragment of 3 John and the latter containing the Pauline epistles. The Dutch Elzevir editions followed next, which were virtually identical to those of the Erasmian-influenced Beza text. It was in the second of seven of these, published in 1633, that there appeared the statement in the preface (in Latin): "You therefore now have the text accepted by everybody, in which we give nothing changed or corrupted." On the continent, this edition became the Textus Receptus or the Received Text. It seems that this success was in no small way due to the beauty and useful size of the Elzevir editions.

In Chapter 2, we will take a moment to look at how and what made the King James Bible so popular that it would be the bestselling Bible for four hundred years. It became so popular that the translation itself became venerated. How did the 1611 King James Version, attain a unique place in the hearts and minds of the English-speaking people?

CHAPTER 2 How the King James Version Became Popular

2011 was the year of the 400th anniversary of the King James version of the Bible, otherwise known as the *Authorized Version*. The English-speaking world was in full celebration. Leland Ryken and Crossway Publishing began the year with the new release *The Legacy of the King James Bible: Celebrating 400 Years of the Most Influential English Translation* (January 5, 2011). There were television and radio specials, documentaries, as well as conferences, lectures, and seminars. King James I of England produced the translation that is noted for its "majesty of style," and has been labeled as one of the most important books in the English history[7] and a driving force that shaped the English-speaking world.[8]

> The King James Bible is a book that attracts superlatives. To David Norton it is "the most important book in English religion and culture," to Gordon Campbell "the most celebrated book in the English-speaking world" and "the most enduring embodiment of Scripture in the English language". To Robert Carroll and Stephen Prickett, it is simply the Bible translation that defines Bible translations: "All other versions still exist, as it were, in its shadow. It has shaped, formed and moulded the language with which the others must speak."[9]

How, though, did the King James Bible attain such a unique place in the hearts and minds of the English-speaking people?

Bible Translation Increases Momentum

Around 1550 there was a yearning for the knowledge of the teachings of the Bible, which had begun to sweep across Europe. John Wycliffe (1330? - 84), a Catholic priest and a professor of theology at Oxford, England had whetted the appetite of English-speaking people almost two centuries earlier, about 1380, with a handwritten translation of the Bible from Latin. Over the next two centuries, the followers of Wycliffe, known as the Lollards, **circulated his Bible texts countrywide**, determined than ever

---

[7] The Times Literary Supplement. 9 February 2011. Archived from the original on 2011-06-17. Retrieved July 30, 2018.

[8] "The King James Bible: The Book That Changed the World - BBC Two". BBC

[9] The Times Literary Supplement. 9 February 2011. Archived from the original on 2011-06-17. Retrieved July 30, 2018.

to keep Wycliffe's work alive. The nickname "Lollard" had its origin going back to the 14th century in the Netherlands. However, Wycliffe died, this name truly came to the fore. It originated from the Middle Dutch lullen (from which we get the English word "lull," archaically meaning to sing, hum or chant), and thus denotes 'a praiser of God.'

Bible scholar and translator William Tyndale's New Testament was yet another breakthrough. The Tyndale Bible was translated from the original Greek language into English by 1525, being the first printed translation. On the heels of Tyndale, Miles Coverdale came out with the complete English Bible in 1535. One year prior to that Henry VIII broke off his relationship with Rome and also made a decisive move. Seeking to strengthen his position as head of the Church of England, Henry VIII commissioned a translation of the Bible into English, which became the first authorized edition of the Bible in English. Because of its immense size (11 inches wide by 16½ inches long in heavy Gothic type), it became known as the Great Bible.

The Puritans and other Protestants, who were exiled from all over Europe settled in Geneva, Switzerland. In 1560 the Geneva Bible, the first English Bible the first Bible to shun the use of Old English Black Gothic type (easy-to-read type) was produced with chapters divided into verses. The Geneva Bible was the first Bible to be printed in a handy size. It was shipped to England from continental Europe and immediately became popular. The Geneva Bible was eventually printed in England as well. Maps, as well as marginal notes, which notes could be found on essentially every page of the Bible, served to help clarify its text. There was some opposition to these notes, however, because they spoke against the papacy.

Overcoming the Difficulties

The Great Bible never really gained widespread acceptance. The Geneva Bible included voluminous hostile footnotes to the papacy. Therefore, a revised Bible was decided upon. the Great Bible was chosen as its foundation. The task was given to Church of England bishops, and in 1568 the Bishops' Bible was published. This two was a large edition, filled with many engravings. However, it too was short-lived and not well-received in England because the Calvinists, who spurned religious titles, objected to the word "bishops."

King James I ascended the English throne in 1603; thereafter, he endorsed the making of a fresh Bible translation. He wanted to make it available to all omitting any offensive notes or comments.

King James backed the project. Ultimately, 47 scholars in six separate groups throughout the country prepared segments of the text. The translation committee made use of Both the Tyndale and the Coverdale Bibles. The Tyndale New Testament was about 84 percent of the text, while in the Old Testament about 76 percent. Most King James Bible users today do not realize that it was a revision of earlier English translations. It was basically a revision of the Bishops' Bible. However, they also used the Geneva Bible and the Roman Catholic Rheims New Testament of 1582.

The **King James Version (KJV)**, also known as the **King James Bible** (KJB) or simply the Authorized **Version** (AV), is an English translation of the Christian **Bible** for the Church of England, begun in 1604 and completed in May of 1611. James himself was a respected Bible scholar, and the translation's dedication acknowledge his leadership, "the most high and mighty prince, James, by the grace of God, king of Great Britain, France, and Ireland, Defender of the Faith, etc." is given credit for having by means of a tract dealt "such a blow to that Man of Sin [meaning the pope] as will not be healed."[10] It was perceived at that time that James, as the head of the Church of England, was seen to be exerting his authority to bring the nation together.

A Literary Masterpiece

The clergy was very pleased to receive this so-called authorized version from the hand of their king. "It was issued in a large folio, in double columns, **with the title** 'The Holy Bible, conteyning the Old Testament, and the New: Newly Translated out of the Originall tongues: and with the former Translations diligently compared and revised by his Maiesties speciall Commandement. Appointed to be read in Churches.' The printer was Robert Barker, London."[11] Yet, even then, how would the nation receive this new translation, seeing that those that came before it never took hold for various reasons.

The translators themselves expressed their apprehension as to its success in an extended preface. The Geneva Bible was the most well received up unto this point; thus, it took 30 years for the King James Bible to displace the Geneva Bible in the affections of the people.

---

[10] William Hendriksen and Simon J. Kistemaker, *Exposition of I-II Thessalonians*, vol. 3, New Testament Commentary (Grand Rapids: Baker Book House, 1953–2001), 174.

[11] Edward Maunde Thompson, *Bible Illustrations* (Oxford; London: Oxford University Press; Henry Frowde, 1896), 38.

The *Cambridge History of the Bible* concludes: "Strictly speaking, the Authorized Version was never authorized, nor were parish churches ordered to procure it. It replaced the Bishops' Bible in public use because after 1611 no other folio Bible was printed. But from Broughton onwards it met with plenty of criticism. In ordinary private use the comprehensive Geneva Bible long competed with it, while scholars and preachers went on using what they would. So strong a Protestant as Becon had continued to quote the Vulgate in Latin or translate directly from it, while at times he took up Tyndale or the Great Bible apparently as it came to hand. Later, so prominent a reviser as Lancelot Andrewes commonly used the Geneva Bible for his sermons, as did other bishops. Eventually, however, its victory [the King James Version] was so complete that its text acquired a sanctity properly ascribable only to the unmediated voice of God; to multitudes of English-speaking Christians it has seemed little less than blasphemy to tamper with the words of the King James Version."[12]

Acts 1:8 "To the Uttermost Part of the Earth"

When the early settlers landed in North America they had the Geneva Bible in hand. However, in time the King James Version would take over and gain far greater acceptance. Moreover, with the expansion of the British Empire throughout the world, so too, Protestant missionaries spread its use. This author is in South America at the time of the writing of this book and I just discovered some very interesting news about the Baptist seminary in Chile, who claim to be of the Southern Baptist Convention position. They only use the Textus Receptus (the text behind the King James Version) and refuse to let their students even use the critical texts WH-NU[13] (the text behind modern translations). The Baptist Church that I attend has a pastor that uses only the King James Version, while his assistant pastor sneaks to use the critical text. Many throughout the last century have translated the Bible into local languages were unfamiliar with Biblical Hebrew and Greek. Therefore, the *King James Version* in English became the source for these local translations.

According to the British Library today, **"The King James Bible remains the most widely published text in the English language.** The official language of the medieval Church was Latin - the language of the Roman Empire. In England, since the early 1400s, it was strictly forbidden to

---

[12] S. L. Greenslade, *The Cambridge History of the Bible, Vol. 3: The West from the Reformation to the Present Day*, (Cambridge University Press, Cambridge, 1975), 168.

[13] Wescott and Hort Critical Text, the Nestle-Aland Critical text, and the United Bible Societies Critical Text.

translate the Bible into English. Tyndale's translation of the bible in 1525 had led to his execution. But by Shakespeare's time, England had split with Rome, and the political scenery had changed. Bibles in English were now available, such as Henry VIII's authorised 'Great Bible'. King James I abolished the death penalty attached to English Bible translation and commissioned a new version that would use the best available translations and sources, and importantly, be free of biased footnotes and commentaries."[14] Some have estimated that the number of copies of the King James Version that have been produced in print worldwide is over one billion!

The Need for Change

There has been a level that runs from devotion to a translation they only know to the other extreme of cult worship of the King James Version. It began with the critical text the Textus Receptus (Latin: "Received Text") behind the New Testament of the King James Version. Desiderius Erasmus' new work was published by Froben of Basel in 1516. It was given such reverence that for several hundred years, even though new original language Greek manuscripts came to light, which dated centuries earlier than the handful of very late Byzantine manuscripts used by Erasmus, no textual scholar dare make corrections to the master Greek text. Harold Greenlee writes, "The Textus Receptus did indeed become the generally received text for nearly three hundred years, as well as the basis for the translation of the early English versions, including the KJV, and various versions in other European languages."[15]

Bruce Metzger writes, "the Textus Receptus lies at the basis of the King James Version and of all the principal Protestant translations prior to 1881. So superstitious has been the reverence accorded the Textus Receptus that in some cases attempts to criticize or emend it has been regarded as akin to sacrilege. Yet, its textual basis is essentially a handful of late and haphazardly collected minuscule manuscripts, and in dozens of passages its rendering is supported by no known Greek witnesses [manuscripts]."[16] In the 19th century, enough time chad passed, so "the influential edition [of the critical Greek Text of the New Testament] prepared by two Cambridge scholars,

---

[14] THE BRISTISH LIBRARY: Learning Timelines: Sources from History (Wednesday, August 01, 2018) http://www.bl.uk/learning/timeline/item102771.html

[15] Greenlee, J. Harold. *The Text of the New Testament: From Manuscript to Modern Edition* (p. 48). Baker Publishing Group.

[16] Bruce Metzger and Bart D. Ehrman, *THE TEXT OF THE NEW TESTAMENT: Its Transmission, Corruption, and Restoration* (4th Edition) (New York, NY: Oxford University Press, 2005), 152.

B. F. Westcott and F. J. A. Hort (1881). It is the latter edition that was taken as the basis for the present United Bible Societies' edition. During the twentieth century, with the discovery of several New Testament manuscripts much older than any that had hitherto been available, it has become possible to produce editions of the New Testament that approximate ever more closely to what is regarded as the wording of the original documents."[17]

In 1881, we have the B. F. Westcott and F. J. A. Hort (1881) master Greek text that displaces the long-revered Textus Receptus. We also have in 1870, work on a full revision of the King James Version started in England. We end up with both the English Revised Version of 1881 and the American Standard Version of 1901. More recent revisions of the King James Version would be the 1952 Revised Standard Version, the 1982 Revised Authorised Version, the 1985 New American Standard Bible, in 1989 the New Revised Standard Version, and the 2001 English Standard Version are all revisions of the King James Version. In 1901, the preface to the American Standard Version said, "We are not insensible to the justly lauded beauty and vigor of the style of the Authorized Version."[18] In 1982, the preface to the Revised Authorised Version said that effort was made "to maintain that lyrical quality which is so highly regarded in the Authorised Version"[19] of 1611. In 1989, the preface to the New Revised Standard Version said, "to summarize in a single sentence: the New Revised Standard Version of the Bible is an authorized revision of the Revised Standard Version, published in 1952, which was a revision of the American Standard Version, published in 1901, which, in turn, embodied earlier revisions of the King James Version, published in 1611."[20]

In 2001, the preface to the English Standard Version said, "The English Standard Version (ESV) stands in the classic mainstream of English Bible translations over the past half-millennium. The fountainhead of that stream was William Tyndale's New Testament of 1526; marking its course were the King James Version of 1611 (KJV), the English Revised Version of 1885 (RV), the American Standard Version of 1901 (ASV), and the Revised Standard Version of 1952 and 1971 (RSV). In that stream, faithfulness to the text and vigorous pursuit of precision were combined with simplicity,

---

[17] Bruce Manning Metzger, United Bible Societies, *A Textual Commentary on the Greek New Testament*, Second Edition a Companion Volume to the United Bible Societies' Greek New Testament (4th Rev. Ed.) (London; New York: United Bible Societies, 1994), xxiv.

[18] American Standard Version (Oak Harbor, WA: Logos Research Systems, Inc., 1995).

[19] The Holy Bible: Revised Authorised Version (Samuel Bagster, 1982).

[20] The Holy Bible: New Revised Standard Version (Nashville: Thomas Nelson Publishers, 1989).

beauty, and dignity of expression. Our goal has been to carry forward this legacy for this generation and generations to come."[21] There is little doubt that the King James Version is a literary masterpiece, which this author has and will appreciate and value for its unparalleled beauty of expression. This book is in no way trying to take away from what the King James Version has accomplished. However, what about the importance of its message? Is it the most accurate translation? Should it be trusted above all others?

From the 1901 American Standard Version to the 1952 Revised Standard Version, to the 1982 Revised Authorised Version, the 1985 New American Standard Bible, and the 2001 English Standard Version, the translation committees and publishers wanted to hold onto the legacy of the King James Version. Yet, these translations all have one thing in common, all made one common significant adjustment. "During the twentieth century [and now twenty-first century], with the discovery of several New Testament manuscripts much older than any that had hitherto been available, it has become possible to produce editions of the New Testament that approximate ever more closely to what is regarded as the wording of the original documents."[22]

A Valuable Modern Translation

This author's primary purpose is to give the Bible readers what God said by way of his human authors, not reverence or even worship of one translation that is itself an admitted revision of other translations in its place, as Truth Matters! The primary goal is to guide the reader to the most accurate and faithful translation, ones that are mirror-like reflections of the originally inspired Word of God. Translating Truth! The Updated American Standard Version will be one of the most faithful and accurate translations to date. www.uasvbible.org/

Chapter 3 will now take on the question found in on many Christian minds whether they use the King James Version or any modern Bible translation. Why have modern Bible translations removed many words, sentences, and verses that are in the King James Bible? When I say this question and the answers are a matter of eternal life and eternal death, it is not hyperbole. The answer begins in Chapter 3.

---

[21] The Holy Bible: English Standard Version (Wheaton: Standard Bible Society, 2016).

[22] Bruce Manning Metzger, United Bible Societies, *A Textual Commentary on the Greek New Testament*, Second Edition a Companion Volume to the United Bible Societies' Greek New Testament (4th Rev. Ed.) (London; New York: United Bible Societies, 1994), xxiv.

CHAPTER 3 Why Have Modern Bible Translations Removed Verses That Are In The King James Version

Many have asked by email and social media,

"In studying the modern Bible translations, I have come across some verses that are left out but that are in my King James Version or even my New King James Version, such as Matthew 18:11; 23:14; Luke 17:36. I have gotten conflicting opinions on social media. Can you please clear this up for me?"

You have likely noticed something similar or have seen this type of discussion on Social media. The importance of the answer is clear, as the book of **Revelation warns:** "if anyone takes away from the words of the book of this prophecy, God will take away his share in the tree of life and in the holy city, which are described in this book." (Rev. 22:19) Clearly, if anyone removes any part of the truly genuine original, inspired, fully inerrant Word of God, it will mean they lose their eternal life. Why did I word it this way? Because the book of **Revelation also warns,** "I warn everyone who hears the words of the prophecy of this book: if anyone adds to them, God will add to him the plagues described in this book." – Revelation 22:18.

Taking Liberties with the Text

What if Luke told us in his truly genuine original, inspired, fully inerrant Word of God in authoring the Gospel of Luke?

Luke 4:8a

And having answered the Jesus said to him
8 καὶ   ἀποκριθεὶς   ὁ Ἰησοῦς εἶπεν   αὐτῷ
It has been written Lord the God of you
Γέγραπται   Κύριον τὸν θεόν   σου
you shall worship and to him alone you will serve.
προσκυνήσεις   καὶ   αὐτῷ   μόνῳ   λατρεύσεις.

TRANSLATION: Jesus answered him, "It is written, 'You shall worship the Lord your God and serve him only.'" (Luke 4:8a)

Now, what if later copyists took liberties with the text and added the following,

And having answered to him the Jesus said
8 καὶ   ἀποκριθεὶς αὐτῷ   ὁ Ἰησοῦς εἶπεν

"Get you behind me Satan It has been written Lord the
"Ὕπαγε ὀπίσω μου, Σατανᾶ   Γέγραπται   Κύριον τὸν

God of you you shall worship and to him alone
θεόν   σου   προσκυνήσεις   καὶ   αὐτῷ   μόνῳ λατρεύσεις.

Luke 4:8a

TRANSLATION: And Jesus answered and said to him, **"Get behind Me, Satan!** For it is written, 'You shall worship the Lord your God, and Him only you shall serve.' " (Luke 4:8a)

Who All Is Accountable, Really?

Now, **if a later copyist** working on the Gospel of Luke knowingly added those words intentionally, he is facing the wrath of Revelation 22:18 for adding to the Word of God.

In addition, if a textual scholar in creating our critical text that Bible translators use in making our translations retains those words, knowing a copyist had added them centuries after Luke authored his original Gospel, he too will suffer the wrath of Revelation 22:18 for adding to the Word of God.

Additionally, if a translator or translation committee in making his translation from the critical text that Bible translators use in making our translations retains those words, knowing a copyist had added them centuries after Luke authored his original Gospel, he too will suffer the wrath of Revelation 22:18 for adding to the Word of God.

Furthermore, if a publisher has the translator or translation committee in making his translation from the critical text that Bible translators use in making our translations retains those words, knowing a copyist had added them centuries after Luke authored his original Gospel, he too will suffer the wrath of Revelation 22:18 for adding to the Word of God.

Finally, if a Bible reader has a preferred Bible translation that they preach from wherein the publisher had the translator or translation committee in making his translation from the critical text that Bible translators use in making our translations retains those words, knowing a copyist had added them centuries after Luke authored his original Gospel, he too will suffer the wrath of Revelation 22:18 for adding to the Word of God.

Now, some might say, you are taking the knowing accountability intent too far and the accountability is with the copyist who added the words centuries after the original if he knowingly did so. Yes, that sounds good but let's look at it from another angle. Suppose a child grew up as a Jehovah's Witness and he loved his life and he really liked the New World Translation they use. Suppose that the child as an adult discovers the truth about the Jehovah's Witnesses and the inaccuracies of the New World Translation. However, because this is all he has known and he likes the lifestyle and does not want to lose his family and friends, he just decides God will not fault him for teaching things from a faulty Bible translation that he knows to be wrong. In his mind, the only people to suffer God's wrath will be the New World Translation committee and the governing body that controls the Jehovah's Witnesses. Now, this is no different than the child that grew up using the King James Version and has become is King James Version Onlyist because he loves the Bible and he does not want to be disowned or ostracized for bringing a modern translation to church.

Keep this in mind if any words, verse, or verses were added by copyists intentionally or unintentionally to the truly genuine original, inspired, fully inerrant Word of God, and later copyists, textual scholars or translators set things back to the truly genuine original, inspired, fully inerrant Word of God, this is not adding to or removing from the Word of God. In other words, the original wording of Luke 4:8a is "And Jesus answered him." Then, a later copyist added "And Jesus answered and said to him, **'Get behind Me, Satan!'"** Then, later textual scholars and translators removed "Get behind Me, Satan!" This put things back to the original. These later translators are not guilty of Revelation 22:19, 'taking away from the words of' God. Only the copyist who **added** knowingly and intentionally, the textual scholar who **retained** knowingly and intentionally, the Bible translation committee who **translated** knowingly, the "Christian" publisher who intentionally **published** knowingly and intentionally, and the "Christians" who have **preached** knowingly and intentionally are guilty of Revelation 22:18, that is, adding to the Word of God.

Let us see how all of this happened. Many words, whole verses, and even many verses have been altered by copyists and intentionally and unintentionally over a 1,400-year period.

Many things did belong in the Bible that was intentionally or unintentionally removed, and many things do not belong in the Bible that were intentionally or unintentionally removed. This is true even if early translations may have included some things. It can be a little disheartening to discover that a Bible translation that has been cherished for over 400-years has retained certain words, phrases, and even whole verses that were not in the truly genuine original, inspired, fully inerrant Word of God.

Before taking a deep dive into these things, be assured that we have critical texts translators use today that are mirror-like reflections of the truly genuine original, inspired, fully inerrant Word of God. In addition, we have many good and very good semi-literal and literal translations. There are no secular writings, like Tacitus, Thucydides or Herodotus, that come even close.

We now have 5,836 Greek New Testament manuscripts, some 66 that date to the first two centuries after the death of the apostle John. These give us a 99.99% certainty of what was originally written. The earlier manuscripts and the more trusted ones help us in determining what has been added later, allowing the honest worker to remove these words, expressions and verses, interpolations, from our modern translations.

In Chapter 4, we want to dispel a common misunderstanding about the early copies of the Greek New Testament of the Alexandrian Textual family being corrupted and that it was the later Byzantine Textual Family that restored and se the text right.

CHAPTER 4 The Trustworthiness of Early Copyists

Throughout much of the twentieth century, it was common to form three conclusions about the earliest copyists and their work:

(1) The first three centuries saw copyists who were semiliterate and unskilled in the work of making copies.

(2) Copyists in these early centuries felt as though the end was nigh, so they took liberties with the text in an attempt to strengthen orthodoxy.

(3) In the early centuries, manuscripts could be described as "free," "wild," "in a state of flux," "chaotic," "a turbid textual morass," i.e., a "free text" (so the Alands).

The first in the above would undoubtedly lead to many unintentional changes while the second would escalate intentional changes. J. Harold Greenlee had this to say:

> In the very early period, the NT writings were more nearly "private" writings than the classics . . . the classics were commonly, although not always, copied by professional scribes, the NT books were probably usually copied in the early period by **Christians who were not professionally trained** for the task, and **no corrector** was employed to check the copyist's work against his exemplar (the MS from which the copy was made) .... It appears that a copyist sometimes even took liberty to add or change minor details in the narrative books on the basis of personal knowledge, alternative tradition, or a parallel account in another book of the Bible .... At the same time, the importance of these factors in affecting the purity of the NT text must not be exaggerated. The NT books doubtless came to be considered as "literature" soon after they began to be circulated, with attention to the precise wording required when copies were made.[23]

Greenlee had not changed his position 14 years later when he wrote the following:

> The New Testament, on the other hand, was probably copied during the earliest period mostly by ordinary Christians

---

[23] J. Harold Greenlee, Introduction to New Testament Textual Criticism (Revised Edition, 1995), 51–52.

who were not professional scribes but who wanted a copy of the New Testament book or books for themselves or for other Christians.[24]

The Alands in their *Text of the New Testament* saw the New Testament books as not being canonical, i.e., not viewed as Scripture in the first few centuries, so the books were subject to changes. They wrote, "not only every church but each individual Christian felt 'a direct relationship to God.' Well into the second century Christians still regarded themselves as possessing inspiration equal to that of the New Testament writings which they read in their worship service." Earlier they wrote, "That was all the more true of the early period when the text had not attained canonical status, especially in the early period when Christians considered themselves filled with the Spirit." They claimed that "until the beginning of the fourth century the text of the New Testament developed freely." (Aland and Aland 1995, 295, 69)

Generally, once an established concept is set within the world of textual scholars, it is not easily displaced. During the start of the 20th century (1900–1930), there was a handful of papyri discovered that obviously represented the work of a copyist who had no training. It is during this time that Sir Frederic Kenyon, director and principal librarian of the British Museum for many years, said,

> The early Christians, a poor, scattered, often **illiterate** body, looking for the return of the Lord at no distant date, **were not likely to care** sedulously for minute accuracy of transcription or to preserve their books religiously for the benefit of posterity.[25]

The first papyri discovered (P[45], P[46], P[66]) showed this to be the case. However, as more papyri became known, especially after the discovery of P[75], it proved to be just the opposite, prompting Sir Frederic Kenyon to write,

> We must be content to know that the general authenticity of the New Testament text has been remarkably supported by the modern discoveries which have so greatly reduced the interval between the original autographs and our earliest extant manuscripts, and that the differences of reading, interesting as

---

[24] J. Harold Greenlee, The Text of the New Testament: From Manuscript to Modern Edition (2008), 37.

[25] F. Kenyon, Our Bible and the Ancient Manuscripts (1895), 157.

they are, do not affect the fundamental doctrines of the Christian faith.[26]

Even though many textual scholars were crediting the Alands' *The Text of the New Testament* with their description of the text as "free," that was not the entire position of the Alands. True, they spoke of the different text styles such as the "normal," "free" "strict" and the "paraphrastic." However, like Kenyon, they saw a need based on the evidence, which suggested a rethinking of how the evidence should be described:

> Our research on the early papyri has yielded unexpected results that require a change in the traditional views of the early text. We have inherited from the past generation the view that the early text was a "free" text, and the discovery of the Chester Beatty papyri seemed to confirm this view. When P[45] and P[46] were joined by P[66] sharing the same characteristics, this position seemed to be definitely established. P[75] appeared in contrast to be a loner with its "strict" text anticipating Codex Vaticanus. Meanwhile the other witnesses of the early period had been ignored. It is their collations which have changed the picture so completely.[27]

While we have said this previously, it bears repeating once again that *some* of the earliest manuscripts we now have indicate that a professional scribe copied them.[28] *Many* of the other papyri confirm that a semi-professional hand copied them, while *most* of these early papyri give evidence of being produced by a copyist who was literate and experienced. Therefore, either literate or semi-professional copyist did the vast majority of our early papyri, with some being done by professionals. As it happened, the few poorly copied manuscripts became known first, establishing a

---

[26] F. Kenyon, Our Bible and the Ancient Manuscripts (1962), 249.

[27] (Aland and Aland, The Text of the New Testament 1995, 93-5)

[28] Some may argue that we can only be confident that we have good manuscripts of an "early" form of the text but not necessarily of the originally published text. This hypothesis cannot be disproven. However, I think it is highly doubtful for four reasons: (1) The intervening time between the publication date of various New Testament books (from AD 60–90) and the date of several of our extant manuscripts (from AD 100–200) is narrow, thereby giving us manuscripts that are probably only three to five "manuscript generations" removed from the originally published texts. (2) We have no knowledge that any of these manuscripts go back to an early "form" that postdates the original publications. (3) We are certain that there was no major Alexandrian recension in the second century. (4) Text critics have been able to detect any other other second-century textual aberrations, such as the D-text, which was probably created near the end of the second century, not the beginning. Thus, it stands to reason that these "reliable" manuscripts are excellent copies of the authorized published texts." (P. Comfort, Encountering the Manuscripts: An Introduction to New Testament Paleography and Textual Criticism 2005, 269)

precedent that was difficult for some to discard when the enormous amount of evidence came forth that showed just the opposite.

Distribution of Papyri by Century and Type					
DATE	ALEX	WEST	CAES	BYZ	Hand
150	P^{52} P^{90} P^{104}	0	0	0	0
200	P^{32} P^{46} $P^{4/64/67}$ P^{66} P^{77} 0189	0	0	0	0
250	P^1 P^5 P^9 P^{12} P^{15} P^{20} P^{22} P^{23} P^{27} P^{28} P^{29} P^{30} P^{39} P^{40} P^{45} P^{47} P^{49} P^{53} P^{65} P^{70} P^{75} P^{80} P^{87} 0220	0	0	P^{48} P^{69}	1
300	P^{13} P^{16} P^{18} P^{37} P^{72} P^{78} P^{115} 0^{162}	0	0	P^{38} 0171	1
Acts	14	0	0	0	4

Also, as we noted earlier, textual scholars such as Comfort[29] and others believe that the very early Alexandrian manuscripts that we now possess are a reflection of what would have been found throughout the whole of the Greco-Roman Empire from about 85–275 C.E. So these early papyri can play a major role in our establishing the original readings.

However, Epp asks, "If Westcott-Hort did not utilize papyri in constructing their NT text, and if our own modern critical texts, in fact, are not significantly different from that of Westcott-Hort, then why are the papyri important after all?"[30] From there, Epp goes on to strongly advise that the papyri should play an essential role in three areas: (1) "to isolate the earliest discernable text-types, (2) assisting "to trace out the very early

---

[29] Philip W. Comfort, The Quest for the Original Text of the New Testament (Eugene, Oregon: Wipf and Stock Publishers, 1992).

[30] The New Testament Papyrus Manuscripts in Historical Perspective, in To Touch the Text: Biblical and Related Studies in Honour of Joseph A. Fitzmyer, S. J. (ed. Maurya P. Horgan and Paul J. Kobelski; New York: Crossroad, 1989), 285 (there italicized) repr. in Epp, Perspectives, 338.

history of the NT text," and, (3) "Finally, the papyri can aid in refining the canons of criticism—the principles by which we judge variant readings—for they open to us a window for viewing the earliest stages of textual transmission, providing instances of how scribes worked in their copying of manuscripts."[31] We should add that the early papyri have changed decisions of textual scholars and committees so that they have not retained the readings of Westcott and Hort at times.

To offer just one example, both Metzger and Comfort inform us that it was the external evidence of the papyri that resulted in the change in the NU text, adopting the reading that was also in the Textus Receptus, as opposed to what was in the Westcott and Hort text.

Matthew 26:20 (WH)	Matthew 26:20 (TRNU)
²⁰ μετα των δωδεκα μαθητων	²⁰ μετα των δωδεκα
With the twelve disciples	With the twelve

Metzger writes, "As is the case in 20:17,[32] the reading μαθηταί after οἱ δώδεκα is doubtful. In the present verse [26:20] the weight of the external evidence seems to favor the shorter reading." (B. M. Metzger, A Textual Commentary on the Greek New Testament 1994, 53) Comfort in his *New Testament Text and Translation* writes, "Even though both P[37] and P[45] are listed as 'vid,' it is certain that both did not include the word μαθητων because line spacing would not accommodate it. P[37] has the typical abbreviation for 'twelve,' as ιβ̄; and P[45] has it written out as [δω]δεκα. P[64+67] is less certain, but line lengths of the manuscript suggest that it reads ιβ̄ (see *Texts of Earliest MSS*, 69)." Comfort more explicitly explains what Metzger hinted at; "The testimony of the papyri (with B and D) created a change in the NU text. Prior to NA26, the NU text included the word μαθητων ("disciples"). But the early evidence shows that this must have been a later addition." Comfort continues, "Such an addition is not necessary in light of the fact that Jesus' closest followers were often

---

[31] Ibid., 288

[32] **20:17** τοὺς δώδεκα [μαθητάς] {C}

Although copyists often add the word μαθηταί to the more primitive expression οἱ δώδεκα (see Tischendorf's note *in loc.* and 26.20 below), a majority of the Committee judged that the present passage was assimilated to the text of Mark (10:32) or Luke (18:31). In order to represent both possibilities it was decided to employ square brackets. (B. M. Metzger, A Textual Commentary on the Greek New Testament 1994, 42)

On 20:17, Comfort writes, "Either reading could be original because they both have good support and because the gospel writers alternated between the nomenclature 'the twelve disciples' and 'the twelve.'" (P. W. Comfort 2008, 60)

designated by the gospel writers as simply "the twelve." (P. W. Comfort 2008, 77)

Again, many textual scholars before 1961 believed that the early copyists of the New Testament papyri were among the untrained in making documents (P[45], P[46], P[47]; P[66] and P[72] in 2 Peter and Jude), and that the papyri were texts in flux.[33] It was not until the discovery of P[75] and other papyri that textual scholars began to think differently. Nevertheless, the attitude of the 1930s through the 1950s is explained well by Kurt and Barbara Aland:

> Of special importance are the early papyri, i.e., of the period of the third/fourth century. As we have said, these have an inherent significance for the New Testament textual studies because they witness to a situation before the text was channeled into major text types in the fourth century. Our research on the early papyri has yielded unexpected results that require a change in the traditional views of the early text. We have inherited from the past generation the view that the early text was a "free" text,[34] and the discovery of the Chester Beatty papyri seemed to confirm this view. When P[45] and P[46] were joined by P[66] sharing the same characteristics, this position seemed to be definitely established. (Aland and Aland 1995, 93)

Before P[75], scholars were under the impression that scribes must have used manuscripts of untrained copyists to make a recension (critical revision, i.e., revised text); and this, according to scholars prior to 1961, was how Codex Vaticanus (B) came about. In 1940, Kenyon inferred the following:

> During the second and third centuries, a great variety of readings came into existence throughout the Christian world. In some quarters, considerable license was shown in dealing with the sacred text; in others, more respect was shown to the tradition. In Egypt, this variety of texts existed, as elsewhere; but

---

[33] Kurt and Barbara Aland write, "By the 1930s the number of known papyri had grown to more than forty without any of them arousing any special attention, despite the fact that many of them were of a quite early date. (Aland and Aland, The Text of the New Testament 1995, 84)

[34] Early manuscripts (from before the fourth century) are classified by the Alands as "strict," "normal," or "free." The "normal" text "transmitted the original text with the limited amount of variation." Then, there is the "free" text, "characterized by a greater degree of variation than the 'normal' text." Finally, there was the "strict" text, "which reproduced the text of its exemplar with greater fidelity (although still with certain characteristic liberties), exhibiting far less variation than the 'normal' text." (Aland 1987, 93)

Egypt (and especially Alexandria) was a country of strong scholarship and with a knowledge of textual criticism. Here, therefore, a relatively faithful tradition was preserved. About the beginning of the fourth century, a scholar may well have set himself to compare the best accessible representatives of this tradition, and so have produced a text of which B is an early descendant.[35]

While Kenyon was correct about the manuscripts coming up out of Egypt being a reasonably pure text, he was certainly mistaken when he suggested that Codex Vaticanus was the result of a critical revision by early scribes. P[75] put this theory to rest. Agreement between P[75] and codex B is 92% in John and 94% in Luke. However, Porter has it at about 85% agreement. Zuntz, on the other hand, went a little further than Kenyon did. Kenyon believed that the critical text had been made in the early part of the fourth century, leading to Codex Vaticanus. Zuntz believed similarly but felt that the recension began back in the mid-second-century and was a process that ran up into the fourth-century. Zuntz wrote:

> The Alexander correctors strove, in ever repeated efforts, to keep the text current in their sphere free from the many faults that had infected it in the previous period and which tended to crop up again even after they had been obelized [i.e., marked as spurious]. These labours must time and again have been checked by persecutions and the confiscation of Christian books, and counteracted by the continuing currency of manuscripts of the older type. Nonetheless they resulted in the emergence of a type of text (as distinct from a definite edition) which served as a norm for the correctors in provincial Egyptian scriptoria. The final result was the survival of a text far superior to that of the second century, even though the revisers, being fallible human beings, rejected some of its own correct readings and introduced some faults of their own.[36]

P[75], as we can see from the above, influenced the thinking of Kurt Aland. While he said, "We have inherited from the past generation the view that the early text was a 'free' text," he was one of those saying that very thing. However, as he would later say, "Our research on the early papyri has yielded unexpected results that require a change in the traditional views of the early text." P[75] greatly affected the Alands: "P[75] shows such a close

---

[35] F. Kenyon, "Hesychius and the Text of the New Testament," in *Memorial Lagrange* (1940), 250.

[36] G. Zuntz, *The Text of the Epistles* (1953), 271–272.

affinity with the Codex Vaticanus that the supposition of a recension of the text at Alexandria, in the fourth century, can no longer be held."[37] Gordon Fee clearly states that there was no Alexandrian recension prior to P[75] (175-225 C.E.) and the time of Codex Vaticanus (350 C.E.), as he commented that P[75] and Vaticanus "seem to represent a 'relatively pure' form of preservation of a 'relatively pure' line of descent from the original text."[38] For many decades now, New Testament textual scholarship has been aware that P[75] is an extremely accurate copy. Of the copyist behind P[75], Colwell said, "his impulse to improve style is for the most part defeated by the obligation to make an exact copy."[39] Colwell went on to comment on the work of that scribe:

> In P[75] the text that is produced can be explained in all its variants as the result of a single force, namely the disciplined scribe who writes with the intention of being careful and accurate. There is no evidence of revision of his work by anyone else, or in fact of any real revision, or check.... The control had been drilled into the scribe before he started writing.[40]

We do not want to leave the reader with the impression that P[75] is perfect, as it is not. On this Comfort says,

> The scribe had to make several corrections (116 in Luke and John), but there was no attempt 'to revise the text by a second exemplar, and indeed no systematic correction at all.'[41] The scribe of P[75] shows a clear tendency to make grammatical and stylistic improvements in keeping with the Alexandrian scriptorial tradition, and the scribe had a tendency to shorten his text, particularly by dropping pronouns. However, his omissions of text hardly ever extend beyond a word or two, probably because he copied letter by letter and syllable by syllable.[42]

---

[37] Kurt Aland, "The Significance of the Papyri for New Testament Research" in *The Bible in Modern Scholarship* (1965), 336.

[38] Gordon Fee, "P75, P66, and Origen: The Myth of Early Textual Recension in Alexandria" in *New Dimensions in New Testament Study* (1974), 19–43.

[39] Ernest C. Colwell, "Method in Evaluating Scribal Habits: A Study of P45, P66, P75," in *Studies in Methodology in Textual Criticism of the New Testament*, New Testament Tools and Studies 9 (Leiden: Brill, 1969), 121.

[40] Ibid., 117

[41] James Ronald Royse, "Scribal Habits in Early Greek New Testament Papyri" (Ph.D. diss., Graduate Theological Union, 1981), 538–39.

[42] (Comfort and Barret, The Text of the Earliest New Testament Greek Manuscripts 2001, 506)

As the early Nestle Greek text moved from edition to edition, the influence of the New Testament papyri increased. It was the son of Eberhard Nestle, Erwin, who added a full critical apparatus in the thirteenth edition of the 1927 Nestle Edition. It was not until 1950 that Kurt Aland began to work on the text that would eventually become known as the Nestle-Aland text. He would begin to add even more evidence from papyri to the critical apparatus of the twenty-first edition. At Erwin Nestle's request, he looked over and lengthened the critical apparatus, adding far more manuscripts. This ultimately led to the 25th edition of 1963. The most significant papyri and recently discovered majuscules, (i.e., 0189), a few minuscules (33, 614, 2814), and rarely also lectionaries were also considered. However, while the critical apparatus was being added to and even altered, the text of the Nestle-Aland was not changed until the 26th edition (1979). Many of these changes to the text were a direct result of the papyri.

Returning to the First Century

The writers of the 27 books comprising the Christian Greek Scriptures were Jews.[43] (Romans 13:1-2) Either these men were apostles, intimate traveling companions of the apostles, or were picked by Christ in a supernatural way, such as the apostle Paul. Being Jewish, they would have viewed the Old Testament as being the inspired, inerrant Word of God. Paul said, "all Scripture is inspired by God" (2 Timothy 3:16). These writers of the 27 New Testament books would have viewed the teachings of Jesus, or their books expounding on his teachings, as Scripture as well as the Old Testament. The teachings of Jesus came to most of these New Testament writers personally from Jesus, being taught orally; thereafter, they would be the ones who published what Jesus had said and taught orally. When it came time to be published in written form, it should be remembered that Jesus had promised them "The Helper, the Holy Spirit, whom the Father will send in my name, he will teach you all things and **bring to your remembrance** all that I have said to you." – John 14:26

The early first-century Christian copyists were very much aware of the traditions that the Jewish scribes followed in meticulously copying their texts. These copyists would have immediately understood that they were

---

[43] Some believe that Luke was a Gentile, basing this primarily on Colossians 4:11, 14. Because Paul first mentioned "the circumcision" (Col 4:11) and thereafter talked about Luke (Col 4:14), the inference is drawn that Luke was not of the circumcision and therefore was not a Jew. However, this is by no means decisive. Romans 3:1-2 says, "Jews were entrusted with the whole revelation of God." Luke is one of those to whom such inspired revelations were entrusted.

copying sacred texts. In fact, the early papyri show evidence of shared features with the Jewish Sopherim, men who copied the Hebrew Scriptures from the time of Ezra in the fifth-century B.C.E. to Jesus' day and beyond. They were extremely careful and were terrified of making mistakes.[44] We will find common features when we compare the Jewish Greek Old Testament with the Christian Greek Scriptures, such things as an enlarged letter at the beginning of each line, and the invention of the nomen sacrum[45] to deal with God's personal name. Marginal notes, accents, breathing marks, punctuation, corrections, double punctuation marks (which indicate the flow of text)–all of these show adoption of scribal practices of the Sopherim by Jewish Christian writers and scribes.

There are, unfortunately, fierce critics who reject any claims of veracity for these early manuscripts. Former evangelical Christian, now agnostic New Testament Bible scholar, Bart Ehrman writes,

> Not only do we not have the originals, we don't have the first copies of the originals. **We don't even have copies of the copies of the originals, or copies of the copies of the copies of the originals.** What we have are copies **made later—much later.** In most instances, they are copies made many *centuries* later. And these **copies all differ from one another, in many thousands of places.** As we will see later in this book, these copies **differ from one another in so many places that we don't even know how many differences** there are. Possibly it is easiest to put it in comparative terms: **there are more differences among our manuscripts than there are words in the New Testament.** (B. D. Ehrman, Misquoting Jesus: The Story Behind Who Changed the Bible and Why 2005, 10) (Bold mine)

As we read these remarks, it is easy to get a sense of hopelessness because "all feels lost, for there is certainly no way to get back to the originals." Correct? Ehrman has had a long history of creating hopelessness for his readers, as he carries on his alleged truth quest. He asserts that even in the very few numbers of places that we might be sure about the *wording*, we cannot be certain about the *meaning*.

---

[44] It is true that they took some liberties with the text, but these few places were the exception to the rule. They intentionally altered some passages that appeared to show irreverence for God or one of his spokespersons.

[45] Nomina sacra (singular: nomen sacrum) means "sacred names" in Latin, and can be used to refer to traditions of abbreviated writing of several frequently occurring divine names or titles in early Greek manuscripts, such as the following:
Lord ($\overline{KC}$), Jesus ($\overline{IH}$, $\overline{IHC}$), Christ ($\overline{XP}$, $\overline{XC}$, $\overline{XPC}$), God ($\overline{\Theta C}$), and Spirit ($\overline{\Pi NA}$).

Blinded by Misguided Perceptions

Ehrman clearly has been immensely impacted by the fact that we do not have the originals or immediate copies. Here we have a world-renowned textual and early Christianity scholar who is emphasizing that we do not have the originals, nor the direct copies, and since there are so many copyist errors, it is virtually impossible to get back to the Word of God at all. Even if by some stroke of fortune, we could, we cannot know the meaning with assurance. Ehrman is saying to the lay reader: we can no longer trust the text of the Greek New Testament as the Word of God. If so, we would have to conclude that all translations are untrustworthy as well.

Ehrman has exaggerated the negative to his readers to the detriment of the positive in New Testament textual criticism. Mark Minnick assesses the latter nicely: "Doesn't the existence of these variants undermine our confidence that we have the very words of God inspired? No! The fact is that because we know of them and are careful to preserve the readings of every one of them, *not one word of God's word has been lost to us.*"[46] The wealth of manuscripts that we have for establishing the original Greek New Testament is overwhelming, in comparison to other ancient literature. We can only wonder what Ehrman does with an ancient piece of literature that has only one copy, and that copy is hundreds or even over a thousand years removed from the time of the original.

Consider a few examples. Before beginning, it should be noted that some of the classical authors are centuries, some many centuries before the first century New Testament era, which is a somewhat unfair comparison. See the chart below.[47]

---

[46] Mark Minnick, "Let's Meet the Manuscripts," in *From the Mind of God to the Mind of Man: A Layman's Guide to How We Got Our Bible,* eds. James B. Williams and Randolph Shaylor (Greenvill, SC: Ambassador-Emerald International, 1999), p. 96.

[47] The concept of this chart is taken from *The Bibliographical Test Updated - Christian Research* ... http://www.equip.org/article/the-bibliographical-test-updated/ May 04, 2017. However, some adjustments have been made as well as footnotes added.

The New Testament Compared to Classical Literature

Author	Work	Writing Completed	Earliest MSS	Years Removed	Number of MSS
Homer	*Iliad*	800 B.C.E.	3rd century B.C.E.[48]	500	1,757
Herodotus	*History*	480–425 B.C.E.	10th cent. C.E.	1,350	109
Sophocles	*Plays*	496–406 B.C.E.	3rd cent. B.C.E.[49]	100-200	193
Thucydides	*History*	460–400 B.C.E.	3rd cent. B.C.E.[50]	200	96
Plato	*Tetralogies*	400 B.C.E.	895 C.E.	1,300	210
Demosthenes	*Speeches*	300 B.C.E.	Fragments from 1st cent. B.C.E.	1,000	340
Caesar	*Gallic Wars*	51-46 B.C.E.	9th cent. C.E.	950	251
Livy	*History of Rome*	59 B.C.E.–17 C.E.	5th cent. C.E.	400	150
Tacitus	*Annals*	100 C.E.	9th-11th cent. C.E.	750–950	33
Pliny, the Elder	*Natural History*	49–79 C.E.	5th cent. C.E. fragment	400	200
Eight Greek NT Authors	27 Books	50 – 98 C.E.	110-125 C.E.	12-27	5,838

The Greek New Testament evidence, as we've mentioned previously, is over 5,838+ Greek manuscripts that have been cataloged, over 9,284 versions, and over 10,000 Latin manuscripts, not to mention an innumerable amount of church fathers' quotations. This places the Greek New Testament in a class by itself, because no other ancient document is close to this. However, there is even more. There are 62 Greek papyri, along with five majuscule manuscripts that date to the second and third centuries C.E. Moreover, these early papyri manuscripts are from a region

---

[48] There are a number of fragments that date to the second century B.C.E. and one to the third century B.C.E., with the rest dating to the ninth century C.E. or later.

[49] Most of the 193 MSS date to the tenth century C.E., with a few fragments dating to the third century B.C.E.

[50] Some papyri fragments date to the third century B.C.E.

in Egypt that appreciated books as literature, and were copied by semi-professional and professional scribes, or at least highly skilled copyists. This region produced what are known as the most accurate and trusted manuscripts.

Were the Scribes in the Early Centuries Amateurs?

>We could **go on nearly forever** talking about specific places in which the texts of the New Testament came to be changed, either accidentally or intentionally. As I have indicated, the examples are **not just in the hundreds but in the thousands**. The examples given are enough to convey the general point, however: there are lots of differences among our manuscripts, differences created by scribes who were reproducing their sacred texts. **In the early Christian centuries, scribes were amateurs** and as such were more inclined to alter the texts they copied—or more prone to alter them accidentally—than were scribes in the later periods who, starting in the fourth century, began to be professionals. (B. D. Ehrman, Misquoting Jesus: The Story Behind Who Changed the Bible and Why 2005, 98) [Bold mine]

Let us take just a moment to discuss Ehrman's statement, "**in the early Christian centuries, scribes were amateurs....**" In this book, we established just the opposite. Literate or semi-professional copyist did the vast majority of our early papyri, with some being done by professionals. As it happened, the few poorly copied manuscripts became known first, establishing a precedent that was difficult for some to discard when the truckload of evidence came forth that showed just the opposite. (P. Comfort 2005, 18-19)

Ehrman is misrepresenting the situation to his readers when he states, "We don't even have copies of the copies of the originals or copies of the copies of the copies of the originals." The way this is worded, he is saying that we do not have copies that are three or four generations removed from the originals. Ehrman cannot know this because we have fifteen copies that are 75 to 100 years removed from the death of the apostle John in 100 C.E. There is the possibility that any of these could be only third or fourth generation removed copies. Furthermore, they could have been copied from a second or third generation. Therefore, Ehrman is misstating the evidence. Moreover, the uncertainty of this rhetoric is exposed by the above fact that we now have "seven New Testament papyri, [which] had recently been discovered, six of them probably from the second century and one of them probably from the first."[51]

Let us do another short review of two very important manuscripts: P[75] and Vaticanus 1209 (B). P[75] is also known as Bodmer 14, 15. As has already been stated, papyrus is writing material used by the ancient Egyptians, Greeks, and Romans that was made from the pith of the stem of a water plant. These are the earliest witnesses to the Greek New Testament. P[75] contains most of Luke and John, dating from 175 C.E. to 225 C.E Vaticanus is designated internationally by the symbol "B" (and 03) and is known as an uncial manuscript written on parchment. It is dated to the mid-fourth-century C.E. [c. 350] and originally contained the entire Bible in Greek. At present, Vaticanus' New Testament is missing parts of Hebrews (Hebrews 9:14 to 13:25), all of First and Second Timothy, Titus, Philemon, and Revelation. Originally, this codex probably had approximately 820 leaves, of which 759 remain.

What kind of weight or evidence do these two manuscripts carry in the eyes of textual scholars? Vaticanus 1209 is a key source for our modern translations. When determining an original reading, this manuscript can stand against other external evidence that would seem to the non-professional to be much more significant. P[75] also is one of the weightiest manuscripts that we have and is virtually identical to Vaticanus 1209, which dates 175 to 125 years later than P[75]. When textual scholars B. F. Westcott and F. J. A. Hort released their critical text in 1881, Hort said that Vaticanus preserved "not only a very ancient text but a very pure line of a very ancient text." (Westcott and Hort, The New Testament in the Original Greek, Vol. 2: Introduction, Appendix 1882, 251) Later scholars argued that Vaticanus was a scholarly recension: a critical revision or edited text. However, P[75] has vindicated Westcott and Hort because of its virtual identity with Vaticanus; it establishes that Vaticanus is essentially a copy of a second-century text, and likely, a copy of the original text, with the exception of a few minor points.

Kurt Aland[52] wrote, "P[75] shows such a close affinity with the Codex Vaticanus that the supposition of a recension of the text at Alexandria, in

---

[51] http://csntm.org/News/Archive/2012/2/10/EarliestManuscriptoftheNewTestamentDiscovered

[52] (1915 – 1994) was Professor of New Testament Research and Church History. He founded the Institute for New Testament Textual Research in Münster and served as its first director for many years (1959–83). He was one of the principal editors of The Greek New Testament for the United Bible Societies.

the fourth century, can no longer be held."[53] David C. Parker[54] says of P[75] that "it is extremely important for two reasons: "like Vaticanus, it is carefully copied; it is also very early and is generally dated to a period between 175 and 225. Thus, it pre-dates Vaticanus by at least a century. A careful comparison between P[75] and Vaticanus in Luke by C.M. Martini demonstrated that P[75] was an earlier copy of the same careful Alexandrian text. It is sometimes called proto-Alexandrian. It is our earliest example of a controlled text, one which was not intentionally or extensively changed in successive copying. Its discovery and study have provided proof that the Alexandrian text had already come into existence in the third century." (Parker 1997, 61) Let us look at the remarks of a few more textual scholars: J. Ed Komoszewski, M. James Sawyer, and Daniel Wallace.

> Even some of the early manuscripts show compelling evidence of being copies of a much earlier source. Consider again Codex Vaticanus, whose text is very much like that of P[75] (B and P75 are much closer to each other than B is to [Codex Sinaiticus]). Yet the papyrus is at least a century older than Vaticanus. When P[75] was discovered in the 1950s, some entertained the possibility that Vaticanus could have been a copy of P[75], but this view is no longer acceptable since the wording of Vaticanus is certainly more primitive than that of P75 in several places.' They both must go back to a still earlier common ancestor, probably one that is from the early second century. (Komoszewski, M. Sawyer and Wallace 2006, 78)

Comfort comments on how we can know that Vaticanus is not a copy of P[75]: "As was previously noted, Calvin Porter clearly established the fact that P[75] displays the kind of text that was used in making codex Vaticanus. However, it is unlikely that the scribe of B used P[75] as his exemplar because the scribe of B copied from a manuscript whose line length was 12–14 letters per line. We know this because when the scribe of Codex Vaticanus made large omissions, they were typically 12–14 letters long.[55] The average line length for P[75] is about 29–32 letters per line.

---

[53] K. Aland, "The Significance of the Papyri for New Testament Research," 336.

[54] Professor of Theology and the Director of the Institute for Textual Scholarship and Electronic Editing at the Department of Theology and Religion, University of Birmingham. Scholar of New Testament textual criticism and Greek and Latin paleography.

[55] Brooke F. Westcott and Fenton J. A. Hort, *Introduction to the New Testament in the Original Greek* (New York: Harper & Bros., 1882; reprint, Peabody, Mass.: Hendrickson, 1988), 233–34.

Therefore, the scribe of B must have used a manuscript like P^{75}, but not P^{75} itself."[56]

Ehrman suggests that the early Christians were not concerned about the integrity of the text, its preservation of accuracy. Let us consult the second-century evidence by way of Tertullian.[57]

> Come now, you who would indulge a better curiosity, if you would apply it to the business of your salvation, run over the apostolic churches, in which the very thrones[58] of the apostles are still pre-eminent in their places,[59] in which their own **authentic writings** are read, uttering the voice and representing the face of each of them severally.[60] (Bold mine)

What did Tertullian mean by "authentic writings"? If he was referring to the Greek originals—and it seems that he was, according to the Latin—it is an indication that some of the original New Testament books were still in existence at the time of his penning this work. However, let us say that it is simply referring to copies that were well-preserved. In any case, this shows that the Christians valued the preservation of accuracy.

We need to visit an earlier book by Ehrman for a moment, *Lost Christianities*, in which he writes, "In this process of recopying the document by hand, what happened to the original of 1 Thessalonians? For some unknown reason, it was eventually thrown away, burned, or otherwise destroyed. Possibly, it was read so much that it simply wore out. The early Christians saw no need to preserve it as the `original' text. They had copies of the letter. Why keep the original?" (B. D. Ehrman 2003, 217)

Here Ehrman is arguing from silence. We cannot read the minds of people today, let alone read the minds of persons 2,000 years in the past. It is a known fact that congregations valued Paul's letters, and Paul exhorted them to share the letters with differing congregations. Paul wrote to the Colossians, and in what we know as 4:16, he said, "And when this letter has been read among you, have it **also read in the church of the Laodiceans;** and see that you also read the letter from Laodicea." The best way to

---

[56] (Comfort and Barret, The Text of the Earliest New Testament Greek Manuscripts 2001)

[57] Tertullian (160 – 220 C.E.), was a prolific early Christian author from Carthage in the Roman province of Africa.

[58] Cathedrae

[59] Suis locis praesident.

[60] Alexander Roberts, James Donaldson and A. Cleveland Coxe, The Ante-Nicene Fathers Vol. III: Translations of the Writings of the Fathers Down to A.D. 325 (Oak Harbor: Logos Research Systems, 1997), 260.

facilitate this would be to send someone to a congregation, have them copy the letter and bring it back to their home congregation. On the other hand, someone could make copies of the letter in the congregation that received it and deliver it to interested congregations. In 1 Thessalonians, the congregation that Ehrman is talking about here, at chapter five, verse 27, Paul says, "I put you under oath before the Lord to **have this letter read to all the brothers**." What did Paul mean by "all the brothers"? It could be that he meant it to be used like a circuit letter, circulated to other congregations, giving everyone a chance to hear the counsel. It may merely be that, with literacy being so low, Paul wanted a guarantee that all were going to get to hear the letter's contents, and he simply meant for every brother and sister locally to have a chance to hear it in the congregation. Regardless, even if we accept the latter, the stress that was put on the reading of this letter shows the weight that these people were placed under concerning Paul's letters.[61] In addition, Comfort comments on how Paul and others would view apostolic letters:

> Paul knew the importance of authorized apostolic letters, for he saw the authority behind the letter that came from the first Jerusalem church council. The first epistle from the church leaders who had assembled at Jerusalem was the prototype for subsequent epistles (see Acts 15). It was authoritative because it was apostolic, and it was received as God's word. If an epistle came from an apostle (or apostles), it was to be received as having the imprimatur [**approval**/authority] of the Lord. This is why Paul wanted the churches to receive his word as being the word of the Lord. This is made explicit in 1 Thessalonians (2:13), an epistle he insisted had to be read to all the believers in the church (5:27). In the Second Epistle to the Thessalonians, Paul indicated that his epistles carry the same authority as his preaching (see 2:15). Paul also told his audience that if they would read what he had written, they would be able to understand the mystery of Christ, which had been revealed to him (see Eph. 3:1–6). Because Paul explained the mystery in his writings (in this case, the encyclical epistle known as "Ephesians"), he urged other

---

[61] The exhortation ἐνορκίζω ὑμᾶς τὸν κύριον ἀναγνωσθῆναι τὴν ἐπιστολὴν πᾶσιν τοῖς ἀδελφοῖς ("I adjure you by the Lord that this letter be read aloud to all the brothers [and sisters]"), is stated quite strongly. ἐνορκίζω takes a double accusative and has a causal sense denoting that the speaker or writer wishes to extract an oath from the addressee(s). The second accusative, in this case τὸν κύριον ("the Lord"), indicates the thing or person by whom the addressees were to swear. The forcefulness of this statement is highly unusual, and in fact it is the only instance in Paul's letters where such a charge is laid on the recipients of one of his letters.—Charles A. Wanamaker, The Epistles to the Thessalonians: A Commentary on the Greek Text (Grand Rapids, Mich.: W.B. Eerdmans, 1990), 208-09.

churches to read this encyclical (see Col. 4:16). In so doing, Paul himself encouraged the circulation of his writings. Peter and John also had publishing plans. Peter's first epistle, written to a wide audience (the Christian diaspora in Pontus, Galatia, Cappadocia, Asia, Bithynia—see 1 Pet. 1:1), was a published work, which must have been produced in several copies from the onset, to reach his larger, intended audience. John's first epistle was also published and circulated—probably to all the churches in the Roman province of Asia Minor. First John is not any kind of occasional epistle; it is more like a treatise akin to Romans and Ephesians in that it contains John's full explanation of the Christian life and doctrine as a model for all orthodox believers to emulate. The book of Revelation, which begins with seven epistles to seven churches in this same province, must have also been inititally published in seven copies, as the book circulated from one locality to the next, by the seven "messengers" (Greek *anggeloi*—not "angels" in this context). By contrast, the personal letters (Philemon, 1 and 2 Timothy, Titus, 2 John, 3 John) were not originally "published"; therefore, their circulation was small. Second Peter also had minimal circulation in the early days of the church. Because of its popularity, the book of Hebrews seemed to have enjoyed wide circulation—this was promoted by the fact that most Christians in the East thought it was the work of Paul and therefore was included in Pauline collections (see discussion below). The book of Acts was originally published by Luke as a sequel to his Gospel (see Acts 1:1–2). Unfortunately, in due course, this book got detached from Luke when the Gospel of Luke was placed in one-volume codices along with the other Gospels.[62]

Peter, as we have seen, also had this to say about Paul's letters: "there are some things in them [Paul's letters] that are hard to understand, which the ignorant and unstable twist to their own destruction, **as they do the other Scriptures**." (2 Pet 3:16) Peter viewed Paul's letters as being on the same level as the Old Testament, which was referred to as Scripture. In the second century (about 135 C.E.), Papias, an elder of the early congregation in Hierapolis, made the following comment.

> I will not hesitate to set down for you, along with my interpretations, everything I carefully learned then from the elders and carefully remembered, guaranteeing their truth. For

---

[62] (P. Comfort, Encountering the Manuscripts: An Introduction to New Testament Paleography and Textual Criticism 2005, 17)

unlike most people I did not enjoy those who have a great deal to say, but those who teach the truth. Nor did I enjoy those who recall someone else's commandments, but those who remember the commandments given by the Lord to the faith and proceeding from the truth itself. In addition, if by chance someone who had been a follower of the elders should come my way, I inquired about the words of the elders--what Andrew or Peter said, or Philip, or Thomas or James, or John or Matthew or any other of the Lord's disciples, and whatever Aristion and the elder John, the Lord's disciples, were saying. For I did not think that information from books would profit me as much as information from a living and abiding voice.[63]

As an elder in the congregation at Hierapolis, in Asia Minor, Papias was an unrelenting researcher, as well as a thorough compiler of information; he exhibited intense indebtedness for the Scriptures. Papias determined properly that any doctrinal statement of Jesus Christ or his apostles would be far more appreciated and respected to explain than the unreliable statements found in the written works of his day. We can compare Jude 1:17, where Jude exhorts his readers to preserve the words of the apostles.

Therefore, the notion that the "early Christians saw no need to preserve it as the 'original' text," is far too difficult to accept when we consider the above. Moreover, imagine a church in middle America being visited by Billy Graham. Now imagine that he wrote them a warm letter, but one also filled with some stern counsel. Would there be little interest in the preservation of those words? Would they not want to share it with others? Would other churches not be interested in it? The same would have been even truer of early Christianity receiving a letter from an apostle like Peter, John, or Paul. There is no doubt that the "original" wore out eventually. However, they lived in a society that valued the preservation of the apostle's words, and it is far more likely that it was copied with care, to share with others, and to preserve. Moreover, let us acknowledge that their imperfections took over as well. Paul would have become a famous apostle who wrote a few churches, and there were thousands of churches toward the end of the first century. Would they have not exhibited some pride in the fact that they received a letter from the famous apostle Paul, who was martyred for the truth? Ehrman's suggestions are reaching and contrary to human nature. It is simply wishful thinking on his part.

---

[63] (Holmes, The Apostolic Fathers: Greek Texts and English Translations 2007, 565)

However, Ehrman may not have entirely dismissed the idea of getting back to the original if he agreed with Metzger in their coauthored fourth edition of *The Text of the New Testament*. Metzger's original comments from previous editions are repeated there as follows.

> Besides textual evidence derived from New Testament Greek manuscripts and from early versions, the textual critic compares numerous scriptural quotations used in commentaries, sermons, and other treatises written by early church fathers. Indeed, so extensive are these citations that if all other sources for our knowledge of the text of the New Testament were destroyed, they would be sufficient alone for the reconstruction of practically the entire New Testament. (Metzger and Ehrman 2005, 126)

How are we to view the patristic citations? Let us look at another book for which Ehrman was coeditor and a contributor with other textual scholars: *The Text of the New Testament in Contemporary Research* (1995). The following is from Chapter 12, written by Gordon Fee (*The Use of the Greek Fathers for New Testament Textual Criticism*).

> In NT textual criticism, patristic citations are ordinarily viewed as the third line of evidence, indirect and supplementary to the Greek MSS, and are often therefore treated as of tertiary importance. When properly evaluated, however, patristic evidence is of primary importance, for both of the major tasks of NT textual criticism: in contrast to the early Greek MSS, the Fathers have the potential of offering datable and geographically certain evidence. (B. D. Ehrman 1995, 191)

To conclude, we have established that Ehrman has painted a picture that is not quite the truth of the matter for the average churchgoer while saying something entirely different for textual scholars. Moreover, he does not help the reader to appreciate just how close the New Testament manuscript evidence is to the time of the original writings, in comparison to manuscripts of other ancient works, many of which are few in number and hundreds, if not a thousand years removed.

In addition, Ehrman has exaggerated the variants in the Greek New Testament manuscripts by **not** qualifying the level of variants. In other words, he has not explained how he counts them to obtain such high numbers. Moreover, Ehrman's unqualified statement, "In the early Christian centuries, scribes were amateurs," has been discredited as well. Either literate or semi-professional copyist did **the vast majority** of the early papyri, with some being done by professionals.

In Chapter 5, we will build on what we have already learned about how the manuscripts came down to us. We will see that manuscripts were separated into families based on where they were copied and what happened once we got the ability to make copies by the printing press as opposed to copying manuscripts by hand. This will mean briefly touching on Desiderius Erasmus again, as he gave us the first publishing printed Greek New Testament text. We will also discuss the period of corruption, which many Bible critics love to discuss but we will also move into the restoration period where hundreds of textual scholars restored the Greek New Testament to its original form through the art and science of what is known as textual criticism.

CHAPTER 5 Manuscripts Separated Into Families Down to The Printed Text of the Greek New Testament

Separated Into Families

We have textual traditions or families of texts, which grew up in a certain region. For example, we have the **Alexandrian text-type**, which Westcott and Hort called the Neutral text that came from Egypt. Then, there is the **Western text-type**, which came from Italy and Gaul as well as North Africa and elsewhere. There was also the **Caesarean text-type**, which came from Caesarea and is characterized by a mixture of Western and Alexandrian readings (B. M. Metzger, A Textual Commentary on the Greek New Testament 1994, Page xxi). The **Byzantine text-type**, also called **Majority Text**, came from Constantinople (i.e., Byzantium).

In short, early Christianity gave rise to what are known as "local texts." Christian congregations in and near cities, such as Alexandria, Antioch, Constantinople, Carthage, or Rome, were making copies of the Scriptures in a form that would become known as their text-type. In other words, manuscripts grew up in certain areas, just like a human family, becoming known as that text-type, having their own characteristics. In reality, it is not as simple as this because there are mixtures of text-types within each text-type. However, generally, each text-type resembles itself more than it does the others. It should also be remembered that most of our extant manuscripts are identical in more than seventy-five percent of their texts. Thus, it is the twenty-five percent of variation that identifies a manuscript as a certain text-type, i.e., what one could call "agreement in error."

Therefore, the process of classifying manuscripts for centuries was to label them a certain text-type, such as Alexandrian, Western, Caesarean, or Byzantine. However, this practice is fading because technology has allowed the textual scholar to carry out a more comprehensive comparison of all readings in all manuscripts, supposedly blurring the traditional classifications. The new method primarily responsible is the Coherence-Based Genealogical Method (CBGM). In this method, an "initial text" is reconstructed that is considered "relatively close to the form of the text from which the textual tradition of a New Testament book has originated." (Stephen C. Carlson)

The original New Testament authors were inspired of God, and error-free. The copyists were not inspired, and errors did show up in the texts as a result. These errors help us to place these texts into certain families. Very early in the transmission process copies of the originals worked their way to these four major religious centers and the copying traditions that distinguish these text-types began to take place. The Alexandrian text-type is the earliest and reflects the work of professional and semi-professional scribes who treated the copying process with respect. The text is simple, without added material, and lacking the grammatical, stylistic polish sometimes imposed by Byzantine scribes. The Western text-type is early second century. These manuscripts reflect the work of scribes that were given to paraphrasing. Scribes freely changed words, phrases, clauses, and whole sentences as they felt it necessary. At times, they were simply trying to harmonize the text, or even add apocryphal material to spice it up. The Caesarean text-type is a mixture of Western and Alexandrian readings. The Byzantine text-type shows the hand of scribes who, as noted, attempted to smooth out both grammar and style, often with a view to making the text easier to understand. These scribes also combined differing readings from other manuscripts that contained variants. The period of 50 to 350 C.E. certainly saw its share of errors (variants) entering into the text, but the era of corruption is the period when the Byzantine text would become the standard text.

The Corruption Period

To round out our understanding of this early history, we need at least a short overview of what happened after 350 C.E. After Constantine legalized Christianity, giving it equal status with the pagan religions, it was much easier to have biblical manuscripts copied. In fact, Constantine ordered 50 copies of the whole of the Bible for the church in Constantinople. Over the next four centuries or so, the Byzantine Empire and the Greek-speaking church were the dominant factors in making the Byzantine text the standard. It was not a matter of its being the better, i.e., more accurate text. From the eighth century forward, the Byzantine text had displaced all others.

After the invention of the Guttenberg printing press in 1455, it would be this Byzantine text which would become the first printed edition by way of Desiderius Erasmus in 1516. Thanks to an advertisement by the publishers it was referred to as the Textus Receptus, or the "Received Text."[64] Over the next four centuries, many textual scholars attempted to make minor

---

[64] (Wilkins) The nuance between "receive" and "accept" is often overlooked in discussing the TR, and the Latin "receptus" could just as well mean "accepted" (i.e. "the text accepted by all"), which I suspect was the intent of the advertisement.

changes to this text based on the development of the science of textual criticism, but to no real effect on its status as the Greek text of the church. Worse still, it would be this inferior text what would lay at the foundation of all English translations until the *Revised English Version* of 1881 and the *American Standard Version* of 1901. It was not until 1881 that two Cambridge scholars, B. F. Westcott and F. J. A. Hort, replaced the Textus Receptus with their critical text. It is this critical edition of the Westcott and Hort text that is the foundation for most modern translations and all critical editions of the Greek New Testament, UBS[5], and the NA[28].

Desiderius Erasmus and the Greek Text

> I WOULD have these words translated into all languages, so that not only Scots and Irish, but Turks and Saracens too might read them . . . I long for the ploughboy to sing them to himself as he follows his plough, the weaver to hum them to the tune of his shuttle, the traveler to beguile with them the dullness of his journey. (Clayton 2006, 230)

Dutch scholar Desiderius Erasmus penned those words in the early part of the 16th century. Like his English counterpart, William Tyndale, it was his greatest desire that God's Word be widely translated and that even the plowboy would have access to it.

Much time has passed since the Reformation, and 98 percent of the world we live in today has access to the Bible. There is little wonder that the Bible has become the bestseller of all time. It has influenced people from all walks of life to fight for freedom and truth. This was especially true during the Reformation of Europe throughout the 16th century. These leaders were of great faith, courage, and strength, such as Martin Luther, William Tyndale, while others, like Erasmus, were more subtle in the changes that they brought. Thus it has been said of the Reformation that Martin Luther only opened the door to it after Erasmus picked the lock.

There is not a single historian of the period who would deny that Erasmus was a great scholar. Remarking on his character, the *Catholic Encyclopedia* says: "He had an unequalled talent for form, great journalistic gifts, a surpassing power of expression; for strong and moving discourse, keen irony, and covert sarcasm, he was unsurpassed." (Vol. 5, p. 514) Consequently, when Erasmus went to see Sir Thomas More, the Lord Chancellor of England, just before Erasmus revealed himself, More was so impressed with his exchange that he shortly said: "You are either Erasmus or the Devil."

The wit of Erasmus was evidenced in a response that he gave to Frederick, elector of Saxony, who asked him what he thought about Martin Luther. Erasmus retorted, "Luther has committed two blunders; he has ventured to touch the crown of the pope and the bellies of the monks." (*Cyclopedia of Biblical, Theological, and Ecclesiastical Literature*: Vol. 3 – p, 279) However, we must ask what type of influence did the Bible have on Erasmus and, in turn, what did he do to affect its future? First, we will look at the early years of Erasmus' life.

Erasmus' Early Life

He was born in Rotterdam, the Netherlands, in 1466. He was not a happy boy, living in a home as the illegitimate son of a Dutch priest. He was faced with the double tragedy of his mother's death at seventeen, and his father shortly thereafter. His guardians ignored his desire to enter the university; instead, they sent him to the Augustinian monastery of Steyn. Erasmus gained a vast knowledge of the Latin language, the classics as well as the Church Fathers. In time, this life was so detestable to him that he jumped at the opportunity, at the age of twenty-six, to become secretary to the bishop of Cambrai, Henry of Bergen, in France. This afforded him his chance to enter university studies in Paris. However, he was a sickly man, suffering from poor health throughout his entire life.

It was in 1499 that Erasmus was invited to visit England. It was there that he met Thomas More, John Colet, and other theologians in London, which fortified his resolution to apply himself to Biblical studies. In order to understand the Bible's message better, he applied himself more fully in his study of Greek, soon being able to teach it to others. It was around this time that Erasmus penned a treatise entitled *Handbook of the Christian Soldier*, in which he advised the young Christian to study the Bible, saying: "There is nothing that you can believe with greater certitude than what you read in these writings." (Erasmus and Dolan 1983, 37)

While trying to escape the plague and make a living in an economy that had bottomed worse than our 20th-century Great Depression, Erasmus found himself at Louvain, Belgium, in 1504. It was there that he fell in love with the study of textual criticism while visiting the Praemonstratensian Abbey of Parc near Louvain. Within the library, Erasmus discovered a manuscript of Italian scholar Lorenzo Valla: *Annotations on the New Testament*. Thereupon Erasmus commissioned to himself the task of restoring the original text of the Greek New Testament.

Erasmus moved on to Italy and subsequently pushed on to England once again. It is this trip that brought to mind his original meeting with

Thomas More, meditating on the origin of More's name (moros, Greek for "a fool"); he penned a satire which he called "Praise of Folly." In this work, Erasmus treats the abstract quality "folly" as a person, and pictures it as encroaching in all aspects of life, but nowhere is folly more obvious than amid the theologians and clergy. This is his subtle way of exposing the abuses of the clergy. It is these abuses that had brought on the Reformation, which was now festering. "As to the popes," he wrote, "if they claim to be the successors of the Apostles, they should consider that the same things are required of them as were practiced by their predecessors." Instead of doing this, he perceived, they believe that "to teach the people is too laborious; to interpret the scripture is to invade the prerogative of the schoolmen; to pray is too idle." There is little wonder that it was said of Erasmus that he had "a surpassing power of expression"! (Nichols 2006, Vol. 2, 6)

The First Greek Text

While teaching Greek at Cambridge University in England, Erasmus continued with his work of revising the text of the Greek New Testament. One of his friends, Martin Dorpius, attempted to persuade him that the Latin did not need to be corrected from the Greek. Dorpius made the same error in reasoning that the "King James Only" people make, arguing: "For is it likely that the whole Catholic Church would have erred for so many centuries, seeing that she has always used and sanctioned this translation? Is it probable that so many holy fathers, so many consummate scholars would have longed to convey a warning to a friend?" (Campbell 1949, 71) Thomas More joined Erasmus in replying to these arguments, making the point that what matters is having an accurate text in the original languages.

In Basel, Switzerland, Erasmus was about to be harassed by the printer Johannes Froben. Froben was alerted that Cardinal Ximenes of Toledo, Spain, had been putting together a Greek and Latin Testament in 1514. However, he was delaying publication until he had the whole Bible completed. The first printed Greek critical text would have set the standard, with any other being all but ignored. Erasmus published his first edition in 1516, while the Complutensian Polyglot (Greek for "many languages") was not issued until 1522.

The fact that Erasmus was terribly rushed resulted in a Greek text that contained hundreds of typographical errors alone.[65] Textual scholar Scrivener once stated: '[It] is in that respect the most faulty book I know' (Scrivener 1894, 185). This comment did not even take into consideration

---

[65] In fact, his copy of Revelation being incomplete, Erasmus simply retranslated the missing verses from the Latin Vulgate back into Greek.

the blatant interpolations into the text that were not part of the original. Erasmus was not oblivious to the typographical errors, which were corrected in a good many later editions. This did not include the textual errors. It was his second edition of 1519 that was used by Martin Luther in his German translation and William Tyndale's English translation. This is exactly what Erasmus wanted, writing the following in that edition's preface: "I would have these words translated into all languages. . . . I long for the ploughboy to sing them to himself as he follows his plough."

Unfortunately the continuous reproduction of this debased Greek New Testament gave rise to its becoming the standard, called the Textus Receptus ("Received Text"), reigning 400 years before it was dethroned by the critical text of B. F. Westcott and F. J. A. Hort in 1881. Regardless of its imperfections, the Erasmus critical edition began the all-important work of textual criticism, which has only brought about a better critical text, as well as more accurate Bible translations.

Erasmus was not only concerned with ascertaining the original words; he was just as concerned with achieving an accurate understanding of those words. In 1519, he penned *Principles of True Theology* (shortened to *The Ratio*). Herein he introduces his principles for Bible study, his interpretation rules. Among them is the thought of never taking a quotation out of its context nor out of the line of thought of its author. Erasmus saw the Bible as a whole work by one ultimate author, and as such it should interpret itself.

Erasmus Contrasted With Luther

Erasmus penned a treatise called *Familiar Colloquies* in 1518, in which again he was exposing corruption in the Church and the monasteries. Just one year earlier, in 1517, Martin Luther had nailed his 95 theses on the church door at Wittenberg, denouncing the indulgences, the scandal that had rocked numerous countries. Many people likely thought that these two could bring about change and reform. This was not going to be a team effort, though, as the two were at opposite ends of the spectrum on how to bring reform about. Luther would come to condemn Erasmus because he was viewed as being too moderate, seeking to make change peacefully within the Church.

The seemingly small bond they may have shared (by way of their writings against the Church establishment) was torn apart in 1524 when Erasmus wrote his essay *On the Freedom of the Will*. Luther believed that salvation results from "justification by faith alone" (Latin, *sola fide*) and not from priestly absolution or works of penance. In fact, Luther was so adamant in his belief of "justification by faith alone" that in his Bible translation, he added the word "alone" to Romans 3:28. What Luther failed to understand was that Paul was writing about the works of the Mosaic Law. (Romans 3:19, 20, 28) Thus, Luther denied the principle that man possesses a free will. However, Erasmus would not accept such faulty reasoning, in that it would make God unjust because this would suggest that man would be unable to act in such a way as to affect his salvation.

As the Reformation was spreading throughout Europe, Erasmus saw complaints from both sides. Many of the religious leaders who supported the reform movement chose to leave the Catholic Church. While they could not predict the result of their decision, they moved forward, many meeting their deaths. This would not be true of Erasmus, though, for he withdrew from the debate, yet he did refuse to be made cardinal. His approach was to try to appease both sides. Thus, Rome saw his writings as being that of a heretic, prohibiting them, while the reformers denounced him as refusing to risk his life for the cause. Here was a man emotionally broken over criticism, but in fear of burning bridges with Rome, so he cautiously sat on the sideline.

The affairs of Erasmus in relation to the Reformation can be summarized as follows: "He was a reformer until the Reformation became a fearful reality; a jester at the bulwarks of the papacy until they began to give way; a propagator of the Scriptures until men betook themselves to the study and the application of them; depreciating the mere outward forms of religion until they had come to be estimated at their real value; in short, a learned, ingenious, benevolent, amiable, timid, irresolute man, who, bearing the responsibility, resigned to others the glory of rescuing the human mind from the bondage of a thousand years. The distance between his career and that of Luther was therefore continually enlarging, until they at length moved in opposite directions, and met each other with mutual animosity."— (McClintock and Strong 1894, 278).

The greatest gain from the Reformation is that the common person can now hold God's Word in his hand. In fact, the English-language person has over 100 different translations from which to choose. From these 16th-century life and death struggles, in which Erasmus shared, there has materialized dependable and accurate Bible translations. Consequently, the "plowboy" of 98 percent of the world can pick up his Bible, or at least part of it.

The Textus Receptus

The Dark Ages (5th to 15th centuries C.E.), was a time when the Church had the Bible locked up in the Latin language, and scholarship and learning were nearly nonexistent. However, with the birth of the Morning Star of the Reformation, John Wycliffe (1328-1384), and the invention of the printing press in 1455, the restraints were loosened, and there was a rebirth of interest in the Greek language. Moreover, with the fall of Constantinople to the Turks in 1453 C. E., many Greek scholars and their manuscripts were scattered abroad, resulting in a revival of Greek in the Western citadels of learning.

About fifty years later, or at the beginning of the sixteenth century, Ximenes, archbishop of Toledo, Spain, a man of rare capability and honor, invited foremost scholars of his land to his university at Alcala to produce a multiple-language Bible—not for the common people, but for the educated. The outcome would be the Polyglot, named Complutensian, corresponding to the Latin of Alcala. This would be a Bible of six large volumes, beautifully bound, containing the Old Testament in four languages (Hebrew, Aramaic, Greek, and Latin) and the New Testament in two (Greek and Latin). For the Greek New Testament, these scholars had only a few manuscripts available to them, and those of late origin. One may wonder why this was the case when they were supposed to have access to the Vatican library. This Bible was completed in 1514, providing the first printed Greek New Testament, but it did not receive approval by the pope to be published until 1520, and was not released to the public until 1522.

Froben, a printer in Basel, Switzerland became aware of the completion of the Complutensian Polyglot Bible and of its pending consent by the pope to be published. Immediately, he saw a prospect of making profits. He at once sent word to Erasmus, who was the foremost European scholar of the day and whose works he had published in Latin, pleading with him to hurry through a Greek New Testament text. In an attempt to bring the first published Greek text to completion, Erasmus was only able to locate, in July of 1515, a few late cursive manuscripts for collating and preparing his text. It would go to press in October of 1515, and would be completed by March of 1516. In fact, Erasmus was in such a hurried mode that he rushed the manuscript containing the Gospels to the printer without first editing it, making such changes as he felt were necessary on the proof sheets. Because of this terrible rush job, the work contained hundreds of typographical errors, as we noted earlier. Erasmus himself admitted this in his preface, remarking that it was "rushed through rather than edited."

Bruce Metzger referred to the Erasmian text as a "debased form of the Greek testament." (B. M. Metzger 1964, 1968, 1992, 103)

As one would expect, Erasmus was moved to produce an improved text in four succeeding editions of 1519, 1522, 1527, and 1535. Erasmus' editions of the Greek text, we are informed, ultimately proved an excellent achievement, even a literary sensation. They were inexpensive, and the first two editions totaled 3,300 copies, in comparison to the 600 copies of the large and expensive six-volume Polyglot Bible. In the preface to his first edition, Erasmus stated, "I vehemently dissent from those who would not have private persons read the Holy Scriptures, nor have them translated into the vulgar tongues." (Baer 2007, 268)

Except for everyday practical consideration, the editions of Erasmus had little to vouch for them, for he had access only to five (some say eight) Greek manuscripts of relatively late origin, and none of these contained the entire Greek New Testament. Rather, these comprised one or more sections into which the Greek texts were normally divided: (1) the Gospels; (2) Acts and the general epistles (James through Jude); (3) the letters of Paul; and (4) Revelation. In fact, of the some 5,750 Greek New Testament manuscripts that we now have, only about fifty are complete.

Consequently, Erasmus had but one copy of Revelation (twelfth-century). Since it was incomplete, he merely retranslated the missing last six verses of the book from the Latin Vulgate back into Greek. He even frequently brought his Greek text in line with the Latin Vulgate; this is why there are some twenty readings in his Greek text not found in any other Greek manuscript.

Martin Luther would use Erasmus' 1519 edition for his German translation, and William Tyndale would use the 1522 edition for his English translation. Erasmus' editions were also the foundation for later Greek editions of the New Testament by others. Among them were the four published by Robert Estienne (Stephanus, 1503-59). The third of these, published by Stephanus in 1550, became the Textus Receptus or Received Text of Britain and the basis for the King James Version. This took place through Theodore de Beza (1519-1605), whose work was based on the corrupted third and fourth editions of the Erasmian text. Beza would produce nine editions of the Greek text, four being independent (1565, 1589, 1588-9, 1598), and the other five smaller reprints. It would be two of Beza's editions, that of 1589 and 1598, which would become the English Received Text.

Beza's Greek edition of the New Testament did not even differ as much as might be expected from those of Erasmus. Why do I say, as might be expected? Beza was a friend of the Protestant reformer, John Calvin, succeeding him at Geneva, and was also a well-known classical and biblical scholar. In addition, Beza possessed two important Greek manuscripts of the fourth and fifth century, the D and D^p (also known as D^2), the former of which contains most of the Gospels and Acts as well as a fragment of 3 John, and the latter containing the Pauline epistles. The Dutch Elzevir editions followed next, which were virtually identical to those of the Erasmian-influenced Beza text. It was in the second of seven of these, published in 1633, that there appeared the statement in the preface (in Latin): "You therefore now have the text accepted by everybody, in which we give nothing changed or corrupted." On the continent, this edition became the Textus Receptus or the Received Text. It seems that this success was in no small way due to the beauty and useful size of the Elzevir editions.

The Restoration Period

For the next 250 years, until 1881, textual scholarship was enslaved to the Erasmian-oriented Received Text. As these textual scholars[66] became familiar with older and more accurate manuscripts and observed the flaws in the Received Text, instead of changing the text, they would publish their findings in introductions, margins, and footnotes of their editions. In 1734, J. A. Bengel of Tübingen, Germany, made an apology for again printing the Received Text, doing so only "because he could not publish a text of his own. Neither the publisher nor the public would have stood for it," he complained. (Robertson 1925, 25)

The first one to break free from this enslavement to the Textus Receptus, in the text itself, was Bible scholar J. J. Griesbach (1745-1812). His principal edition comes to us in three volumes, the first in Halle in 1775-7, the second in Halle and London in 1796-1806, and the third at Leipzig in 1803-7. However, Griesbach did not fully break from the Textus Receptus. Nevertheless, Griesbach is the real starting point in the development of classifying the manuscripts into families, setting down principles and rules for establishing the original reading, and using symbols to indicate the degree of certainty as to its being the original reading. We will examine his contributions in more detail below.

Karl Lachmann (1793-1851) was the first scholar fully to get out from under the influence of the Textus Receptus. He was a professor of ancient

---

[66] Brian Walton (1600-61), Dr. John Fell (1625-86), John Mill 1645-1707), Dr. Edward Wells (1667-1727), Richard Bentley (1662-1742), John Albert Bengel (1687-1752), Johann Jacob Wettstein (1693-1754), Johann Salomo Semler (1725-91), William Bowyer Jr. (1699-1777), Edward Harwood (1729-94), and Isaiah Thomas Jr. (1749-1831).

classical languages at Berlin University. In 1831, he published his edition of the Greek New Testament without any regard to the Textus Receptus. As Samuel MacAuley Jackson expressed it: Lachmann "was the first to found a text wholly on ancient evidence; and his editions, to which his eminent reputation as a critic gave wide currency, especially in Germany, did much toward breaking down the superstitious reverence for the textus receptus." Bruce Metzger had harsh words for the era of the Textus Receptus as well:

> So superstitious has been the reverence accorded the Textus Receptus that in some cases attempts to criticize it or emend it have been regarded as akin to sacrilege. Yet its textual basis is essentially a handful of late and haphazardly collected minuscule manuscripts, and in a dozen passages its reading is supported by no known Greek witnesses. (B. M. Metzger 1964, 1968, 1992, 106)

Subsequent to Lachmann came Friedrich Constantine von Tischendorf (1815-74), best known for his discovery of the famed fourth-century Codex Sinaiticus manuscript, the only Greek uncial manuscript containing the complete Greek New Testament. Tischendorf went further than any other textual scholar to edit and made accessible the evidence contained in leading as well as less important uncial manuscripts. Throughout the time that Tischendorf was making his valuable contributions to the field of textual criticism in Germany, another great scholar, Samuel Prideaux Tregelles (1813-75) in England made other valued contributions. Among them, he was able to establish his concept of "Comparative Criticism." That is, the age of a text, such as Vaticanus 1209, may not necessarily be that of its manuscript (i.e. the material upon which the text was written), which was copied in 350 C.E., since the text may be a faithful copy of an earlier text, like the second-century P[75]. Both Tischendorf and Tregelles were determined defenders of divine inspiration of the Scriptures, which likely had much to do with the productivity of their labors. If you take an opportunity to read about the lengths to which Tischendorf went in his discovery of Codex Sinaiticus, you will be moved by his steadfastness and love for God's Word.

The Climax of the Restored Text

The critical text of Westcott and Hort of 1881 has been commended by leading textual scholars over the last one hundred and forty years, and still stands as the standard. Numerous additional critical editions of the Greek text came after Westcott and Hort: Richard F. Weymouth (1886), Bernhard Weiss (1894–1900); the British and Foreign Bible Society (1904,

1958), Alexander Souter (1910), Hermann von Soden (1911–1913); and Eberhard Nestle's Greek text, *Novum Testamentum Graece*, published in 1898 by the Württemberg Bible Society, Stuttgart, Germany. The Nestle in twelve editions (1898–1923) to subsequently be taken over by his son, Erwin Nestle (13th–20th editions, 1927–1950), followed by Kurt Aland (21st–25th editions, 1952–1963), and lastly, it was coedited by Kurt Aland and Barbara Aland (26th–27th editions, 1979–1993).

Many of the above scholars gave their entire lives to God and the Greek text. Each of these could have an entire book devoted to them and their work alone. The amount of work they accomplished before the era of computers is nothing short of astonishing. Rightly, the preceding history should serve to strengthen our faith in the authenticity and general integrity of the Greek New Testament. Unlike Bart D. Ehrman, men like Sir Frederic Kenyon have been moved to say that the books of the Greek New Testament have "come down to us substantially as they were written." And all this is especially true of the critical scholarship of the almost two hundred years since the days of Karl Lachmann, due to which all today can feel certain that what they hold in their hands is a mirror reflection of the Word of God that was penned in twenty-seven books, some two thousand years ago.

Chapter 6 will take another look at the accusations that the modern translations have removed verses.

CHAPTER 6 Modern Bible Translations Have Been Accused of Removing Words, Phrases, Sentences, Who Verses, Even Whole Sections

The Warning

Deuteronomy 4:2; 12:32 Updated American Standard Version (UASV)

[2] You shall not add to the word which I am commanding you, nor take away from it, that you may keep the commandments of Jehovah your God which I command you. [32] "Everything that I command you, you shall be careful to do; you shall not add to nor take away from it.

Revelation 22:18-19 Updated American Standard Version (UASV)

[18] I testify to everyone who hears the words of the prophecy of this book: if anyone adds to them, God will add to him the plagues which are written in this book; [19] and if anyone takes away from the words of the book of this prophecy, God will take away his part from the tree of life and out of the holy city, which are written in this book.

These are the verses that the King James Version Onlyist use to misinform the King James Version reader. First, it is true that if one removes a part of the Bible that was in the originals, it would be a catastrophic mater for that person or persons. Second, I would argue, as would the modern-day translators, that Luke 17:36 under discussion herein, as well as Matthew 18:11; 23:14 were not in the originals, they were added by later copyists, who are actually the ones who added to God's Word and so, they face the above judgment. Third, I would further point out that you cannot add what was never there in the first place. Let us see why the modern-day Bibles are not lacking these verses. Because this may be the first time some are hearing that there are certain words, phrases, sentences, even whole verses that are found in the King James Version and other older translations that are not authentic, i.e., they were not in the original.

Before we begin, let's make it clear that the entire Bible that we have today, the critical translation of the Hebrew Old Testament and the Greek New Testament are mirror-like reflections of the originals. All translations that remain faithful to the original are reliable. New Testament textual scholars have over 5,836+ Greek manuscripts, not to mention ancient versions such as Latin, Coptic, Syriac, Armenian, Georgian, and Gothic, which number into the tens of thousands. We have many early and reliable manuscripts in Greek and the versions, a good number that cover almost the entire New Testament dating within 100 years of the originals. Therefore, reconstructing the original Greek New Testament is not only realistic but is now a reality.

Copying Manuscripts

Some are still not aware that no Bible translator has had access to the originals of the New Testament when making their translations because they have not been in existence for almost 2,000 years. Even if they were discovered, we could never ascertain that they were the originals unless they were autographed by Matthew, Mark, Luke, John, James, Peter, or Jude. Almost immediately after the originals were written, copies were being made to be used by the early Christian church.

We have inherited from the past generation the view that the early text was a 'free' text, and the discovery of the Chester Beatty papyri seemed to confirm this view. When P^{45} and P^{46} were joined by P^{66} sharing the same characteristics, this position seemed to be definitely established. P^{75} appeared in contrast to be a loner with its "strict" text anticipating Codex Vaticanus. Meanwhile, the other witnesses of the early period had been ignored. It is their collations which have changed the picture so completely.[67]

While we have said this once, it bears repeating, as *some* of the earliest manuscripts that we now have evidence that a professional scribe copied them. *Many* of the other papyri confirm that a semiprofessional hand copied them, while *most* of these early papyri give evidence of being produced by a copyist who was literate and experienced. Therefore, either literate or semiprofessional copyist did the vast majority of the early extant papyri, with some being done by professionals. As it happened, the few poorly copied manuscripts became known first, establishing a precedent that was difficult for some to shake when the enormous amount of evidence emerged that showed just the opposite.

The most reliable of the earliest texts are P^1, $P^{4, 64, 67}$, P^{23}, P^{27}, P^{30}, P^{32}, P^{35}, $P^{39, P49, 65}$, P^{70}, P^{75}, P^{86}, P^{87}, P^{90}, P^{91}, P^{100}, P^{101}, P^{106}, P^{108}, P^{111}, P^{114}, and P^{115}. The copyists of these manuscripts allowed very few variants in their copies of the exemplars. They had the ability to make accurate judgments as they went about their copying, resulting in superior texts. Whether their skills in copying were a result of their belief that they were copying a sacred text,

---

[67] (Aland and Aland, The Text of the New Testament 1995, 93-5)

or from their training, cannot be known. It could have been a combination of both. These papyri are of great importance when considering textual problems and are considered by many textual scholars to be a good representation of the original wording of the text that was first published by the biblical author. Still, "many of these manuscripts contain singular readings and some 'Alexandrian' polishing, which needs to be sifted out." (P. Comfort 2005, 269) Nevertheless, again, they are the best texts and the most faithful in preserving the original. While it is true that some of the papyri are mere fragments, some contain substantial portions of text. We should note too that text types really did not exist per se in the second century, and it is a mere convention to refer to the papyri as Alexandrian, since the best Alexandrian manuscript, Vaticanus, did exist in the second century by way of P^{75}. It is not that the Alexandrian text existed, but rather P^{75}/Vaticanus evidence that some very strict copying with great care was taking place. Manuscripts that were not of this caliber of strict and careful copying were the result of scribal errors and scribes taking liberties with the text. Therefore, even though P^5 may be categorized as a Western text-type, it is more a matter of negligence in the copying process.

"What we do know, from the manuscript evidence, is that several of the earliest Christian scribes were well-trained scribes who applied their training to making reliable texts, both of the Old Testament and the New Testament. We know that they were conscientious to make a reliable text in the process of transcription (as can be seen in manuscripts like $P^{4+64+67}$ and P^{75}), and we know that others worked to rid the manuscript of textual corruption. This is nowhere better manifested than in P^{66}, where the scribe himself and the *diorthotes* (official corrector) made over 450 corrections to the text of John. As is explained in the next chapter, the *diorthotes* of P^{66} probably consulted other exemplars (one whose text was much like that of P^{75}) in making his corrections. This shows a standard Alexandrian scriptoral practice at work in the reproduction of a New Testament manuscript." (P. Comfort, Encountering the Manuscripts: An Introduction to New Testament Paleography and Textual Criticism 2005, 264)

Scribes Taking Liberties

While we can say that the early Alexandrian copyists certainly made some mistakes at times and added some intentional changes, generally, they used extreme care to make certain that their work was an exact duplication of the exemplar (archetype; master copy) that they were copying. Metzger tells us of another family of manuscripts, "The *Byzantine text,* otherwise called the *Syrian text* (so Westcott and Hort), …, on the whole, the latest of the several distinctive types of text of the New Testament. It is characterized chiefly by lucidity and completeness. The framers of this text sought to smooth away any harshness of language, to combine two or more divergent readings into one expanded reading (called conflation), and to harmonize divergent parallel passages. This conflated text, produced perhaps at Antioch in Syria, was taken to Constantinople, whence it was distributed widely throughout the Byzantine Empire."[68]

It went something like this, a scribe who was very familiar with the Gospel of Matthew, as he is going about the work of copying the Gospel of Mark or Luke, had a tendency to to pen the wording that he had memorized from Matthew. Another way these interpolations crept into the text was carried out unintentionally as well. The scribe who is familiar with the Gospels may take note that a sentence that Matthew used was not to be found in Mark or Luke, so the scribe decides to add the sentence into the margin. However, a later copyist using this manuscript as his exemplar might not know if the sentence that has been added to the margin is there because it should be in the main text, so he moves the sentence from the margin to the main text in his copy of Mark or Luke, as it makes the accounts agree more closely. For example, In Luke's account of the Lord's Prayer, some manuscripts (A C D W Θ Ψ 070 f^{13} 33^{vid} Maj it syr^{c,h,p} cop) add "Our Father who is in heaven"[69] (Luke 11:2a) Also, in Luke 11:2b, which should read "let your kingdom come," some manuscripts (D it^d) expand it to, "let your kingdom come **upon us**."[70] In addition, in Luke 11:2c, some manuscripts (ℵ A C D W Θ Ψ 070 f 33 Maj it syr$^{.p}$ cop^{bo}) add "let your will be done on earth as it is in heaven," which is not present in (P^{75} B L syr^c, Marcion Origen).[71] The weightier manuscript evidence suggests that this interpolation was taken from Matthew 6:10. These harmonizations were interpolations from sincerely motivated scribes with good intentions.

The Dark Ages (5th to 15th centuries C.E.), was a time when the Church had the Bible locked up in the Latin language, and scholarship and learning were nearly nonexistent. However, with the birth of the Morning Star of

---

[68] Bruce Manning Metzger, United Bible Societies, *A Textual Commentary on the Greek New Testament, Second Edition a Companion Volume to the United Bible Societies' Greek New Testament (4th Rev. Ed.)* (London; New York: United Bible Societies, 1994), xxi.

[69] Philip W. Comfort, *New Testament Text and Translation Commentary: Commentary on the Variant Readings of the Ancient New Testament Manuscripts and How They Relate to the Major English Translations* (Carol Stream, IL: Tyndale House Publishers, Inc., 2008), 202.

[70] IBID., 202.

[71] IBID., 203.

the Reformation, John Wycliffe (1328-1384), and the invention of the printing press in 1455, the restraints were loosened, and there was a rebirth of interest in the Greek language. Moreover, with the fall of Constantinople to the Turks in 1453 C. E., many Greek scholars and their manuscripts were scattered abroad, resulting in a revival of Greek in the Western citadels of learning. Now, let us jump ahead to the 16th century, just prior to the plethora of English translations that were to come on the scene. After the invention of the Guttenberg printing press in 1455, it would be this Byzantine text which would become the first printed edition by way of Desiderius Erasmus in 1516. Thanks to an advertisement by the publishers it was referred to as the Textus Receptus, or the "Received Text." The Scriptures had been locked up in the Latin language for a thousand years and now scholars began to demand copies in Greek, the language in which the New Testament was written.

About fifty years later, or at the beginning of the sixteenth century, Ximenes, archbishop of Toledo, Spain, a man of rare capability and honor, invited foremost scholars of his land to his university at Alcala to produce a multiple-language Bible—not for the common people, but for the educated. The outcome would be the Polyglot, named Complutensian, corresponding to the Latin of Alcala. This would be a Bible of six large volumes, beautifully bound, containing the Old Testament in four languages (Hebrew, Aramaic, Greek, and Latin) and the New Testament in two (Greek and Latin). For the Greek New Testament, these scholars had only a few manuscripts available to them, and those of late origin. One may wonder why this was the case when they were supposed to have access to the Vatican library. This Bible was completed in 1514, providing the first printed Greek New Testament, but it did not receive approval by the pope to be published until 1520 and was not released to the public until 1522.

Froben, a printer in Basel, Switzerland became aware of the completion of the Complutensian Polyglot Bible and of its pending consent by the pope to be published. Immediately, he saw a prospect of making profits. He at once sent word to Erasmus, who was the foremost European scholar of the day and whose works he had published in Latin, pleading with him to hurry through a Greek New Testament text. In an attempt to bring the first published Greek text to completion, Erasmus was only able to locate, in July of 1515, a few late cursive manuscripts for collating and preparing his text. It would go to press in October of 1515 and would be completed by March of 1516. In fact, Erasmus was in such a hurried mode that he rushed the manuscript containing the Gospels to the printer without first editing it, making such changes as he felt were necessary on the proof sheets. Because of this terrible rush job, the work contained hundreds of typographical errors, as we noted earlier. Erasmus himself admitted this in his preface, remarking that it was "rushed through rather than edited." Bruce Metzger referred to the Erasmian text as a "debased form of the Greek Testament." (B. M. Metzger 1964, 1968, 1992, 103)

Froben had asked Erasmus to put a rush on a Greek copy of the New Testament. Erasmus was given an extremely short notice to get done, in haste, what should have taken a couple of years at a minimum. With only a half dozen manuscripts (Byzantine), with just one being moderately old and only slightly reliable. Erasmus went to work with none of the manuscripts containing the entire New Testament, Moreover, some verses were not even in this handful of manuscripts. Therefore, Erasmus had to actually translate the verses that had initially been translated from Greek into Latin back into Greek. There is no manuscript out of the 5,836+ that we have that contain this part of the Textus Receptus.

Martin Luther would use Erasmus' 1519 edition for his German translation, and William Tyndale would use the 1522 edition for his English translation. Erasmus' editions were also the foundation for later Greek editions of the New Testament by others. Among them were the four published by Robert Estienne (Stephanus, 1503-59). The third of these, published by Stephanus in 1550, became the Textus Receptus or Received Text of Britain and the basis for the King James Version. This took place through Theodore de Beza (1519-1605), whose work was based on the corrupted third and fourth editions of the Erasmian text. Beza would produce nine editions of the Greek text, four being independent (1565, 1589, 1588-9, 1598), and the other five smaller reprints. It would be two of Beza's editions, that of 1589 and 1598, which would become the English Received Text.

Beza's Greek edition of the New Testament did not even differ as much as might be expected from those of Erasmus. Why do I say, as might be expected? Beza was a friend of the Protestant reformer, John Calvin, succeeding him at Geneva, and was also a well-known classical and biblical scholar. In addition, Beza possessed two important Greek manuscripts of the fourth and fifth century, the D and D^p(also known as D^2), the former of which contains most of the Gospels and Acts as well as a fragment of 3 John, and the latter containing the Pauline epistles. The Dutch Elzevir editions followed next, which were virtually identical to those of the Erasmian-influenced Beza text. It was in the second of seven of these, published in 1633, that there appeared the statement in the preface (in Latin): "You therefore now have the text accepted by everybody, in which we give nothing changed or corrupted." On the continent, this edition became the Textus Receptus or the Received Text. It seems that this success was in no small way due to the beauty and useful size of the Elzevir editions.

Why should this brief history of our Greek New Testament be so important to us? How can our knowing that Erasmus created the first printed master Greek text with chiefly two corrupt twelfth-century manuscripts help us today, some 500 years after 1516? The reason that it is important to us is because of the impact Erasmus' master Greek text had.

The fact that Erasmus was terribly rushed resulted in a Greek text that contained hundreds of typographical errors alone.[72] Textual scholar Scrivener once stated: '[It] is in that respect the most faulty book I know' (Scrivener 1894, 185). This comment did not even take into consideration the blatant interpolations into the text that were not part of the original. Sir Frederic Kenyon made this observation about the Textus Receptus, "The result is that the text accepted in the sixteenth and seventeenth centuries, to which we have clung from a natural reluctance to change the words which we have learnt as those of the Word of God, is in truth full of inaccuracies, many of which can be corrected with absolute certainty from the vastly wider information which is at our disposal today."[73] Erasmus was not oblivious to the typographical errors, which were corrected in a good many later editions. This did not include the textual errors. It was his second edition of 1519 that was used by Martin Luther in his German translation and William Tyndale's English translation.

The Restoration Period Reiterated for Emphasis

For the next 250 years, until 1881, textual scholarship was enslaved to the Erasmian-oriented Received Text. As these textual scholars[74] became familiar with older and more accurate manuscripts and observed the flaws in the Received Text, instead of changing the text, they would publish their findings in introductions, margins, and footnotes of their editions. In 1734, J. A. Bengel of Tübingen, Germany, made an apology for again printing the Received Text, doing so only "because he could not publish a text of

---

[72] In fact, his copy of Revelation being incomplete, Erasmus simply retranslated the missing verses from the Latin Vulgate back into Greek.

[73] Frederic G. Kenyon Sr., Our Bible and the Ancient Manuscripts: Being a History of the Text and Its Translations (London: Eyre & Spottiswood, 1896), 162.

[74] Brian Walton (1600-61), Dr. John Fell (1625-86), John Mill 1645-1707), Dr. Edward Wells (1667-1727, Richard Bentley (1662-1742), John Albert Bengel (1687-1752), Johann Jacob Wettstein (1693-1754), Johann Salomo Semler (1725-91), William Bowyer Jr. (1699-1777), Edward Harwood (1729-94), and Isaiah Thomas Jr. (1749-1831)

his own. Neither the publisher nor the public would have stood for it," he complained. (Robertson 1925, 25)

The first one to break free from this enslavement to the Textus Receptus, in the text itself, was Bible scholar J. J. Griesbach (1745-1812). His principal edition comes to us in three volumes, the first in Halle in 1775-7, the second in Halle and London in 1796-1806, and the third at Leipzig in 1803-7. However, Griesbach did not fully break from the Textus Receptus. Nevertheless, Griesbach is the real starting point in the development of classifying the manuscripts into families, setting down principles and rules for establishing the original reading, and using symbols to indicate the degree of certainty as to its being the original reading. We will examine his contributions in more detail below.

Karl Lachmann (1793-1851) was the first scholar fully to get out from under the influence of the Textus Receptus. He was a professor of ancient classical languages at Berlin University. In 1831, he published his edition of the Greek New Testament without any regard to the Textus Receptus. As Samuel MacAuley Jackson expressed it: Lachmann "was the first to found a text wholly on ancient evidence; and his editions, to which his eminent reputation as a critic gave wide currency, especially in Germany, did much toward breaking down the superstitious reverence for the textus receptus." Bruce Metzger had harsh words for the era of the Textus Receptus as well:

> So superstitious has been the reverence accorded the Textus Receptus that in some cases attempts to criticize it or emend it have been regarded as akin to sacrilege. Yet its textual basis is essentially a handful of late and haphazardly collected minuscule manuscripts, and in a dozen passages its reading is supported by no known Greek witnesses. (B. M. Metzger 1964, 1968, 1992, 106)

Subsequent to Lachmann came Friedrich Constantine von Tischendorf (1815-74), best known for his discovery of the famed fourth-century Codex Sinaiticus manuscript, the only Greek uncial manuscript containing the complete Greek New Testament. Tischendorf went further than any other textual scholar to edit and made accessible the evidence contained in leading as well as less important uncial manuscripts. Throughout the time that Tischendorf was making his valuable contributions to the field of textual criticism in Germany, another great scholar, Samuel Prideaux Tregelles (1813-75) in England made other valued contributions. Among them, he was able to establish his concept of "Comparative Criticism." That is, the age of a text, such as Vaticanus 1209, may not necessarily be that of its manuscript (i.e. the material upon which the text was written), which was copied in 350 C.E., since the text may be a faithful copy of an earlier text, like the second-century P^{75}. Both Tischendorf and Tregelles were determined defenders of divine inspiration of the Scriptures, which likely had much to do with the productivity of their labors. If you take an opportunity to read about the lengths to which Tischendorf went in his discovery of Codex Sinaiticus, you will be moved by his steadfastness and love for God's Word.

The Climax of the Restored Text

The critical text of Westcott and Hort of 1881 has been commended by leading textual scholars over the last one hundred and forty years, and still stands as the standard. Numerous additional critical editions of the Greek text came after Westcott and Hort: Richard F. Weymouth (1886), Bernhard Weiss (1894–1900); the British and Foreign Bible Society (1904, 1958), Alexander Souter (1910), Hermann von Soden (1911–1913); and Eberhard Nestle's Greek text, *Novum Testamentum Graece*, published in 1898 by the Württemberg Bible Society, Stuttgart, Germany. The Nestle in twelve editions (1898–1923) to subsequently be taken over by his son, Erwin Nestle (13th–20th editions, 1927–1950), followed by Kurt Aland (21st–25th editions, 1952–1963), and lastly, it was coedited by Kurt Aland and Barbara Aland (26th–27th editions, 1979–1993).

Many of the above scholars gave their entire lives to God and the Greek text. Each of these could have an entire book devoted to them and their work alone. The amount of work they accomplished before the era of computers is nothing short of astonishing. Rightly, the preceding history should serve to strengthen our faith in the authenticity and general integrity of the Greek New Testament. Unlike Bart D. Ehrman, men like Sir Frederic Kenyon have been moved to say that the books of the Greek New Testament have "come down to us substantially as they were written." And all this is especially true of the critical scholarship of the almost two hundred years since the days of Karl Lachmann, due to which all today can feel certain that what they hold in their hands is a mirror reflection of the Word of God that was penned in twenty-seven books, some two thousand years ago.

Even though dozens of others had given their lives to the restoration of the Greek New Testament text, the pinnacle of those efforts came in the late 19th century with B. F. Westcott and F. J. A. Hort, who produced a restored text in 1881 that has been widely accepted. Westcott and Hort carried out their work so meticulously and thoroughly, possessing such knowledge insight, and skill that all textual scholars since then has been working in reaction to their work. This restored text of Westcott and Hort has been the basis for almost all modern-day translations. On this Metzger writes,

> Subsequently other critical editions appeared, including those prepared by Constantin von Tischendorf, whose eighth edition (1869–72) remains a monumental thesaurus of variant readings, and the influential edition prepared by two Cambridge scholars, B. F. Westcott and F. J. A. Hort (1881). **It is the latter edition that was taken as the basis for the present United Bible Societies' edition.** During the twentieth century, with the discovery of several New Testament manuscripts much older than any that had hitherto been available, it has become possible to produce editions of the New Testament that approximate ever more closely to what is regarded as the wording of the original documents.[75] (Bold mine)

Some Verses That Should Not Have Ever Been

Matthew 17:21 King James Version (KJV)	Matthew 17:21 Updated American Standard Version (UASV)
²¹ Howbeit this kind goeth not out but by prayer and fasting.	²¹ ——[196]

Many later Greek manuscripts add vs 21, scribes making it agree with Mark 9:29, [But this kind does not go out except by prayer and fasting.] However, the earliest, weightiest, and diverse manuscripts ℵ* B Θ 0281 33 892* it^e Sy^{c,s} cop^{sa} WHNU does not contain vs 21.

Matthew 18:11 King James Version (KJV)	Matthew 18:11 Updated American Standard Version (UASV)
¹¹ For the Son of man is come to save that which was lost.	¹¹ ——[202]

---

[75] Bruce Manning Metzger, United Bible Societies, *A Textual Commentary on the Greek New Testament, Second Edition a Companion Volume to the United Bible Societies' Greek New Testament (4th Rev. Ed.)* (London; New York: United Bible Societies, 1994), xxiv.

The earliest and most trusted two manuscripts (א B) do not include variant 1 or variant 2. Also excluding these variants is L* Θ* f¹· 33 itᵉ syrˢ copˢᵃ Origen as well. Multiple later manuscripts (D L W Θᶜ 078 Maj syrᶜ·ᵖ) ad variant 1: "For the Son of Man has come to save that which was lost." Several other manuscripts (Lᵐᵍ 892ᶜ itᶜ syrʰ) would expand upon this reading in variant 2: "For the Son of Man came to seek and to save the lost." Based on their not being in the most important and trusted witnesses and diverse witnesses (Alexandrian, Egyptian, Antiochian), clearly, variant 1 and variant 2 are interpolations (spurious) were not part of the original. It seems that the copyists inserted this verse in the text to create some sort of bridge between Matthew 18:10 and 18:12, so they borrowed it from Luke 19:10, which is not even parallel to this one. In all likelihood, the shorter variant came first, and a later copyist expanded upon it with the longer variant 2, bringing it to the point where it corresponds exactly with Luke 19:10.

Matthew 23:14 King James Version (KJV)	**Matthew 23:14** Updated American Standard Version (UASV)
¹⁴ Woe unto you, scribes and Pharisees, hypocrites! for ye devour widows' houses, and for a pretence make long prayer: therefore ye shall receive the greater damnation.	¹⁴ —[247]

This verse was taken from Mark 12:40 or Luke 20:47 and inserted **before** verse 13 of Matthew Chapter 24 in the *Majority Text* (W 0102 0107 it syrʰ·ᵖ) but **after** verse 13 in the *Textus Receptus* (f¹³ it syrᶜ). It was not in the original text of Matthew per it not being in the early weighty documentary witnesses against the reading from the Alexandrian and Western text types. (א B D L Z Θ f¹ 33 it·ᵉ syrˢ copˢᵃ) This type of harmonization of the gospels was common after the fourth century CE and is characteristic of the Byzantine text-type. Both the KJV and the NKJV part company with the Textus Receptus and instead went with the Majority Text when they placed the verse after verse 13. Many modern-day translations cite the verse in a footnote out of respect for its long history in the English Bible. The HCSB and the NASB take it to the next level out of reverence for the KJV and the NKJV readers, so they place this interpolation right in the main text within square brackets with footnotes that read, "Other mss omit bracketed text" and "This v not found in early mss" respectively. However, it should be noted that the 2017 CSB removed this spurious verse from the main text. The HCSB and the NASB are not helping their readers by clinging to a translation that is based on corrupt, inferior manuscripts support.

Mark 7:16 King James Version (KJV)	Mark 7:16 Updated American Standard Version (UASV)
¹⁶ If any man have ears to hear, let him hear.	¹⁶ ——[41]

WH NU ℵ B L Δ * 0274 al omit; A D W Θ f¹·¹³ 33 Maj, "If anyone has ears to hear, let him hear." The scribe clearly added this verse from 4:9 or 4:23, as it is nearly identical, possibly seeking to provide an ending for a short pericope.

Mark 9:44, 46 King James Version (KJV)	Mark 9:44, 46 Updated American Standard Version (UASV)
⁴⁴ Where their worm dieth not, and the fire is not quenched. ⁴⁶ Where their worm dieth not, and the fire is not quenched.	⁴⁴ ——[53] ⁴⁶ ——[55]

WH NU ℵ B C L W ΔΨ 0274 f¹ 28 565 itᵏ syrˢ cop omit; A D Θ f¹³ Maj, "where their worm does not die and the fire is not quenched." This verse is identical to verse 48 and is missing from the earliest and best manuscripts, as well as several text types. It is an interpolation.

WH NU ℵ B C L W ΔΨ 0274 f¹ 28 565 itᵏ syrˢ cop omit; A D Θ f¹³ Maj, "where their worm does not die and the fire is not quenched." This verse is identical to verse 48 and is missing from the earliest and best manuscripts, as well as several text types. It is an interpolation.

Mark 11:26 King James Version (KJV)	Mark 11:26 Updated American Standard Version (UASV)
²⁶ But if ye do not forgive, neither will your Father which is in heaven forgive your trespasses.	²⁶ ——[63]

Many later Greek manuscripts added vs 26, as the scribes were expanding on verse 25, inserting the words from Matt. 6:15 making it agree with its parallel account. [But if you do not forgive, neither will your Father who is in the heavens forgive your trespasses.] However, the omission has much stronger manuscript support: ℵ B L W Δ Ψ 565 700 syr^s WH NU omit vs 26.

Mark 15:28 King James Version (KJV)	**Mark 15:28** Updated American Standard Version (UASV)
²⁸ And the scripture was fulfilled, which saith, And he was numbered with the transgressors.	²⁸ ——[93]

WH NU omit verse, which is supported by the earliest and best manuscripts ℵ A B C D Ψ it^k syr^s cop^{sa}. A variant/TR add verse Και επληρωθη η γραφη η λεγουσα· και μετα ανομων ελογισθη "And the Scripture was fulfilled that says, 'He was counted among the lawless,'" which is supported by L Θ 083 0250 f^{1,13} Maj syr^{h,p}.

Luke 17:36 King James Version (KJV)	**Luke 17:36** Updated American Standard Version (UASV)
³⁶ Two men shall be in the field; the one shall be taken, and the other left.	³⁶—[134]

The earliest and most reliable manuscripts (P^{75} ℵ A B L W Δ Θ Ψ f^1 33 cop$^{.bo}$) does not contain 17:36, while later manuscripts (D f 700 it syr) does contain verse 36, "Two men will be in the field; one will be taken and the other will be left." This is likely a scribal interpolation taken from Matthew 24:40. This verse is missing from Tyndale's version (1534) and the Geneva Bible (1557). Even the King James Version translators had their doubts about 17:36, as it reads in the original 1611 edition and a sidenote in good quality editions today, "This 36th verse is wanting in most of the Greek copies."

John 5:3b-4 King James Version (KJV)	**John 5:3b-4** Updated American Standard Version (UASV)
³ In these lay a great multitude of impotent folk, of blind, halt, withered, waiting for the moving of the water. ⁴ For an angel went down at a certain season into the pool, and troubled the water: whosoever	³ In these lay a multitude of sick ones, blind, lame, and paralyzed. ⁴—[29]

then first after the troubling of the water stepped in was made whole of whatsoever disease he had.	

The earliest and best witnesses (P⁶⁶ P⁷⁵ ℵ B C D L T Wˢ 33 579 1241 it syᶜ co) **do not have** John 5:3b-4 in their exemplar; Other later witnesses (Aᶜ C³ D K Wˢ Γ Δ Θ Ψ 078 $f^{1.13}$ 33. 565. 579. 700. 892. 1241. 1424 Maj lat syᵖ·ʰ boᵖᵗ) did contain: "waiting for the moving of the water. ⁴ For an angel of the Lord would come down at certain seasons into the pool and stirred the water. Whoever went in first after the stirring of the water was healed of whatever disease he had." This interpolation was added by later scribes to explain the sick man's answer in verses 7 where he describes 'the water being stirred up.'

Acts 8:37 King James Version (KJV)	Acts 8:37 Updated American Standard Version (UASV)
³⁷ And Philip said, If thou believest with all thine heart, thou mayest. And he answered and said, I believe that Jesus Christ is the Son of God.	³⁷—[22]

The earliest and best Greek manuscripts (P⁴⁵· ⁷⁴ ℵ A B C) as well as 33 81 614 vg syrᵖ·ʰ copˢᵃ·ᵇᵒ eth Chrysostom Ambrose do not contain vs 37, while other manuscripts 4ᵐᵍ (E 1739 it syrʰ** Irenaeus Cyprian) contain, And Philip said, "If you believe with all your heart, you may." And he replied, "I believe that Jesus Christ is the Son of God." If this were apart of the original, there is no good reason why it would be missing in so many early witnesses and versions. This is a classic example of a scribe taking liberties with the text by answering the Eunuch's question ("Look! Water! What prevents me from being baptized?") with ancient Christian baptismal practices from a later age.

Acts 15:34 King James Version (KJV)	Acts 15:34 Updated American Standard Version (UASV)
³⁴ Notwithstanding it pleased Silas to abide there still.	³⁴—[128]

Verse 34 is not contained in the earliest and diverse manuscripts (P⁷⁴ ℵ A B E Ψ Maj syrᵖ copᵇᵒ), while vs 34 is contained in two different forms in other manuscripts (C 33 614 1739 syr** copˢᵃ) "But it seemed good to Silas to remain there" and (P[127vid] D it[.w]) "But it seemed good to Silas to remain with them, so Judas traveled alone." The scribes likely incorporated a gloss from the margin that was trying to rationalize why Silas just happened to be there in verse 40 for the apostle Paul to choose him as a traveling companion. The only problem is that the interpolation of vs 34 contradicts vs 33.

Acts 24:6b–8a King James Version (KJV)	Acts 24:6b–8a Updated American Standard Version (UASV)
⁶ Who also hath gone about to profane the temple: whom we took, and would have judged according to our law. ⁷ But the chief captain Lysias came upon us, and with great violence took him away out of our hands, ⁸ Commanding his accusers to come unto thee: by examining of whom thyself mayest take knowledge of all these things, whereof we accuse him.	⁶ He even tried to desecrate the temple, but we seized him. ⁷ ——[254] ⁸ When you examine him yourself, you will find out about all these things of which we are accusing him."

P[74] ℵ A B H L P 049 cop omit the following from vss 6-8, which read, according to (E) Ψ Maj 33 614 1739 it (syr): "We wanted to judge him according to our own Law. ⁷ But Lysias the commander came along, and with much violence took him out of our hands, ⁸ ordering his accusers to come before you." The earliest and most reliable manuscripts have the shorter reading. The interpolation is a classic example of a scribe trying to fill in what he perceives to be gaps in the text.

Acts 28:29 King James Version (KJV)	Acts 28:29 Updated American Standard Version (UASV)
²⁹ And when he had said these words, the Jews departed, and had great reasoning among themselves.	²⁹ —[287]

The earliest and best Greek manuscripts (P[74] ℵ A B E Ψ 048 33 1739 syr[p] cop) do not contain vs 29, while is later less trusted manuscripts (Maj it syr[h**]) that contain Acts 28:29, "When he had spoken these words, the

Jews departed, having a great dispute among themselves." This is another example of later scribes seeking to fill in the narrative where they perceive there is a gap in the account.

Romans 16:24 King James Version (KJV)	Romans 16:24 Updated American Standard Version (UASV)
²⁴ The grace of our Lord Jesus Christ be with you all. Amen.	²⁴ ——[112]

The earliest and best manuscripts (P⁴⁶ P⁶¹ ℵ A B C 1739 It^b cop) do not contain vs 24, while later witnesses (D Ψ Maj syr^h) contain 16:24, "The grace of our Lord Jesus Christ be with you all. Amen," with F G omitting Ιησου Χριστου [Jesus Christ]. This verse is the same as the end of vs 20. All modern translations do not include this verse because of the superior testimony against it.

1 John 5:7-8 King James Version (KJV)	1 John 5:7-8 Updated American Standard Version (UASV)
⁷ For there are three that bear record in heaven, the Father, the Word, and the Holy Ghost: and these three are one. ⁸ And there are three that bear witness in earth, the Spirit, and the water, and the blood: and these three agree in one.	⁷ For there are three that testify:[16] ⁸ the Spirit and the water and the blood; and the three are in agreement.

The earliest and best manuscripts (ℵ A B (Ψ) Maj syr cop arm eth it) do not contain this spurious interpolation. Only eight late Greek manuscripts add "... in heaven, the Father, the Word, and the Holy Spirit, and these three are one. ⁸ And there are three that testify on earth, the Spirit." If this passage had been in the original, there is no good reason why it would have been removed either accidentally or intentionally. None of the Greek church fathers quote this passage, which they certainly would have during the Trinitarian controversy. (Sabellian and Arian). This interpolation is not in any of the ancient versions, such as Syriac, Coptic, Armenian, Ethiopic, Arabic, Slavonic, and the Old Latin in its early form, or Jerome's Latin Vulgate. Intrinsically, the interpolation "makes an awkward break in the sense" as Metzger points out.

Some other verses that contain interpolations (italics is the spurious portion) are **Matthew 20:16 (*b*) KJV:** ¹⁶ ... *for many be called, but few chosen.* **Mark 6:11 (*b*) KJV:** ¹¹ And whosoever shall not receive you, nor hear you, when ye depart thence, shake off the dust under your feet, for a testimony against them: *Verily I say unto you, it shall be more tolerable for Sodom and Gomorrah in the Day of Judgement, than for that city.* ¹² And they went out, and preached ... **Luke 4:8 (*b*) KJV:** ⁸ And Jesus answered and said unto to him [the Devil], "*Get thee behind me, Satan, for* it is written, ..." **Luke 23:17 KJV:** *For of necessity he must release one unto them at the feast.* **Acts 9:5-6 KJV:** ⁵ And he [Paul] said, 'Who art thou Lord?' and the Lord said, 'I am Jesus whom thou persecutest. *It is hard for thee to kick against the pricks.'* ⁶ *And he, trembling and astonished, said, 'Lord, what wilt thou have me to do?' And the Lord said unto him,* 'Arise, and go into the city, and it shall be told thee what thou must do.'

Translation Chart from Wikipedia

O = omitted in main text.

B = bracketed in the main text – The translation team and most biblical scholars today believe were not part of the original text. However, these texts have been retained in brackets in the NASB and the Holman CSB.[140]

F = omission noted in the footnote.

Passage	NIV	NASB	NKJV	NRSV	ESV	HCSB	NET	NLT	WEB
			Bible Translations						
Matthew 9:34									
Matthew 12:47				F	F	F		F	
Matthew 17:21	F	B	F	O	F	B	O	F	

Matthew 18:11	F	B	F	O	F	B	O	O
Matthew 21:44			F	F		B		F
Matthew 23:14	F	B	F	O	F	B	O	O
Mark 7:16	F	B	F	O	F	B	O	O
Mark 9:44	F	B	F	O	F	B	O	O
Mark 9:46	F	B	F	O	F	B	O	O
Mark 11:26	F	B	F	O	F	B	O	O
Mark 15:28	F	B	F	O	F	B	O	O
Mark 16:9–20	B	B	F	F	B	B	B	
Luke 17:36	F	B	F	O	F	B	O	O	F
Luke 22:20					F		F	
Luke 22:43		B	F	F		B	B	F
Luke 22:44		B	F	F		B	B	F
Luke 23:17	F	B	F	O	F	B	O	O
Luke 24:12								
Luke 24:40				F				

John 5:4	F	B	F	O	F	B	O	O	
John 7:53–8:11	B	F	F	B	B	B			
Acts 8:37	F	B	F	F	F	B	O	O	F
Acts 15:34	F	B	F	O	F	O	O	O	F
Acts 24:7	F	B	F	O	F	B	O	O	F
Acts 28:29	F	B	F	O	F	B	O	O	
Romans 16:24	F	B	F	O	F	B	O	O	

As was mentioned above, some scribes have added a sentence or even an entire verse from elsewhere to another part of the manuscript he was copying. This is clearly made evident in Mark 9:43-48. In the above Bible translations, you can see that verses 44 and 46 are omitted in the main text with the omission noted in the footnote. The only exception in the NASB and the HCSB, which bracketed 44 and 46 in the main text. These translation committees and most biblical scholars today believe verses 44 and 46 were not part of the original text. It could be the translation committees are clinging to the King James Version readers. The text of verses 44 and 46 reads, "where their worm does not die, and the fire is not quenched," the same as in verse 48.

Mark 9:44: WH NU ℵ B C L W ΔΨ 0274 f¹ 28 565 it^k syr^s cop omit; A D Θ f¹³ Maj, "where their worm does not die and the fire is not quenched." This verse is identical to verse 48 and is missing from the earliest and best manuscripts, as well as several text types. It is an interpolation.

Mark 9:46: WH NU ℵ B C L W ΔΨ 0274 f¹ 28 565 it^k syr^s cop omit; A D Θ f¹³ Maj, "where their worm does not die and the fire is not quenched." This verse is identical to verse 48 and is missing from the earliest and best manuscripts, as well as several text types. It is an interpolation.

Clearly, as the evidence suggests a scribe or scribes simply repeated verse 48. This could have been intentional or unintentional. Therefore, when modern translations remove verse 44 and 46; they are not removing part of God's Word because (1) it was never a part of God's Word in the first place and (2) the same sentence is right there in verse 48 of the same account. However, what are these translations accomplishing by removing these two spurious interpolations? The text is being restored to what Mark had been inspired to write.

Looking again at our example verse above, we note that there are other cases where the verses come not from the same book but from another book of the Bible. There are generally footnotes that help the reader to see this but often, the translations do not give the reader enough information so he or she can fully understand. If you compare your King James Version with the modern translations, you will discover that the verse that has been omitted, it is merely a verse repeated from another place in that book or another Bible book. If we look at Romans 16:24 again, we will see that the earliest and best manuscripts (P⁴⁶ P⁶¹ ℵ A B C 1739 It^b cop) do not contain vs 24, while later witnesses (D Ψ Maj syr^h) contain 16:24, "The grace of our Lord Jesus Christ be with you all. Amen," with F G omitting Ιησου Χριστου [Jesus Christ]. This verse is the same as the end of vs 20. All modern translations do not include this verse because of the superior testimony against it. When we compare 16:24 with 16:20 and the closing passages in almost any of the books written by the apostle Paul, we discover that at Romans 16:24, some scribe plainly added a closing expression that is identical to or very similar to the conclusion in almost all of Paul's books.

Trusting the Greek New Testament

As we have looked at a few verses that obviously were not part of the original inspired text that the author penned, this should not leave us doubting the trustworthiness of God's Word. We should not that 90% of the Hebrew Old Testament Text is without significant variation and 93% of the Greek New Testament Text is without significant variation. We have the work of hundreds of textual scholars from the days of Desiderius Erasmus, who have given their entire lives to the restoration of the Greek New Testament. Therefore, textual scholars only need to focus their attention on this very small 07% of significant textual variants. These variants that have been corrected have not undermined the Word of God, rather they highlight and stress the fact that God has preserved his Word through restoration.

Chapter 7 deals with providing insights into the King James Version that most readers are not aware. What do most readers of the King James Bible not know about the translation that they use?

CHAPTER 7 Do You Really Know the King James Version?

"Willful blindness (sometimes called ignorance of law, willful ignorance or contrived ignorance or Nelsonian knowledge) is a term used in law to describe a situation in which a person seeks to avoid civil or criminal liability for a wrongful act by intentionally keeping himself or herself unaware of facts that would render him or her liable."[76] This is the case with many of the King James Version readers, who are known as the King James Version Only. The King James Version Only followers, as we might call them, they are willfully blind, in that they intentionally keep themselves and others unaware of facts from how the Bible came down to us from the original Hebrew Old Testament and Greek New Testament manuscripts, to the copyists of these books of the Bible, to the early version, and finally the translations that would enable them to be fully informed.

---

[76] Criminal Law – Cases and Materials, 7th ed. 2012, Wolters Kluwer Law & Business; John Kaplan, Robert Weisberg, Guyora Binder, - Wikipedia.

For example, you have the so-called Pastor and Bible Teacher Mark Wright[77] of an online Bible School. Richling states that the King James Bible is not "the final authority," as most King James Only believers commonly proffer. Rather, Wright goes on to say, "that is a lie that is not true, the King James Bible is all authority. You see if it is the final authorities leading up to it and that is simply not the case. There is no authority leading up to the Word of God and the Word of God ends up being the final authority. No, the King James Bible is all authority. That's what God says in his book." This would seem to suggest that even the inspired authors of God's Word are not the true authority but only the King Kames Bible. While Mark Wright is an extreme example, going beyond the King James Only group, they are not far behind.

What most of these King James Only readers and those who simply prefer the King James Bible do not know about this translation. Many readers of the King James Bible argue most about other translations that supposedly changed the Bible by taking things out of the Bible. First, it is not removing words, phrases, sentences, and whole verses from the Bible, if they were never in the original to start with but were added later by copyists who took intentional liberties with the text or accidentally altered the original language texts. Those who argue that the modern translations of the Bible are guilty of changing the Bible (what they mean changing the King James Version), they do not know that the King James Version has already been changed in thousands of ways?

A common joke among those who are aware of how the Bible came down to us is the attempt by King James Version Only readers in their defense of the King James Bible, they often say, "If the Authorized Version was good enough for St. Paul, it is good enough for me." First, we would note that Paul lived 1,500 years before the King James Bible came into existence and the English language itself was not even in existence in Paul's day. The truth is the King James version is used by more of the English-speaking world than any other single translation. As we have shown, it is so esteemed that many persons revere, even worship it as the only true Bible.

These countless Millions who use the King James version believe that it is satanic or rather that it is Satan who is responsible with the modern-day translations keep rolling off the presses. The KJVO pastors, priests, and ministers are the ones, who propagate this line. The irony is that the average churchgoer, as well as most church leadership, has no idea of the history of the King James Version itself let along all other aspects of God's Word: such

---

[77] The name has been changed

as the Old Testament and New Testament manuscripts, the early versions, the translations before the King James Version or anything that took place after 1611. They do not even know what illuminating document is probably missing from their own copies of the King James Bible. Sadly, they do not even know their own King James Bible.

God himself is the author of the sixty-six books that we call the Bible, wherein he used 40+ human authors, as he moved them along by the Holy Spirit. The original manuscripts by these inspired authors were inerrant, infallible, without error. This is not true of the copyist thereafter or the translators. What is the purpose of Bible translation? It is to take the thoughts of God, originally written in Hebrew, Aramaic, and Greek, and put them into the current languages of today, such as English. It was for this reason that the Tyndale, Coverdale, the Great Bible, the Geneva Bible, the Bishop's Bible and the King James Version came into existence. That latter was in 1611.

Early English Bible History

Earlier we learned how many English translations of the Bible had come into being. There was the first handwritten translation by **John Wycliffe** in 1380. **Martin Luther** would translate the New Testament into German for the first time from the corrupt 1516 Greek-Latin New Testament of **Desiderius Erasmus** and publish it in September of 1522. **William Tyndale** wanted to use the same 1516 Erasmus text (Textus Receptus) as a source to translate and print the first New Testament into English for the first time in history. Tyndale came to Luther's in Germany in 1525, and by the end of the year, he had translated the New Testament into English. For his efforts, Tyndale was incarcerated for almost one and half years before he was strangled and burned at the stake in 1536. **Miles Coverdale** finished his translation work the Old Testament, and in 1535 he printed the first complete Bible in the English language. Thus, the first complete English Bible was printed on October 4, 1535, and became known as the Coverdale Bible. Just three years later in 1539 King Henry funded the printing of an English Bible known as the **Great Bible.** Then, we had the Geneva Bible of 1560 and the Bishops' Bible of 1568.

Some 36 years later, King James I started the translation project that would bring us the King James Version. It would not be a translation from the Original but rather it would be a revision of the versions then in use. This is evident from the instructions given by King James to the translators. They were to use the Bishop's Bible with the instruction to not deviate from it as little as possible. If Tyndale's, Matthew's, Coverdale's, Whitchurch's, and the Geneva Bible agreed over and against the Bishop's Bible, it was to be the preferred reading. In 1611, a new translation emerged on the scenes, basically ended up being the Tyndale-Coverdale text and some improved alterations from the KJV translators themselves. These improvements focused particularly on the choice of words and enrichment of the rhythmic quality of the text. The result was a version that was superior to its predecessors as to the accuracy of translation and the refinement of literary style. Were the church leaders and churchgoers of 1611 rejoicing over the fact that they had a superior, more accurate translation of God's Word, giving them God's thoughts more correctly than all of the numerous previous English translations?

The Irony of It All

Even before the publication of this new and improved translation, the King James Version, was final, it faced opposition. Why? The church leaders and the churchgoers were quite familiar with and happy with the English translations that they had been using, feeling as though they already had a trusted translation of God's thoughts. The people preferred to keep the translations that they were already familiar with and trusted. These church leaders and churchgoers lost sight of the whole purpose of the Bible itself. Paul tells us at 2 Timothy 3:16-17, "All Scripture is inspired by God and profitable for teaching, for reproof, for correction, for training in righteousness; so that the man of God may be fully competent, equipped for every good work." Certainly, being familiar with, trusting and preferring the Geneva Bible is not keeping in mind the purpose of God's Word and the purpose of translating in the first place. The irony is that here we are defending the improved translation work of the King James Version over its predecessors, previous English translations, from Bible readers of 1611 that wanted to retain a translation (e.g., the Geneva Bible) that they preferred because it was familiar to them; thus, they trusted it.

From almost every quarter the King James Bible was being hammered with opposition. Criticism was frequently severe. Hugh Broughton (1549 – 1612) was an English scholar of Hebrew and a theologian of the day, who wrote King James, where he criticized the new translation unsparingly, saying that he "would rather be torn asunder by wild horses than allow such a version to be imposed on the church."[78] The King James Version translators were unaware that the people of 1611 preferred to keep the translations that they had already grown familiar with, but they were well

---

[78] Robert Burns Wallace, *An Introduction to the Bible as Literature* (London, England, UK: Westminster Press, 1929), 299.

aware that their translation work had unleashed a storm. They attempted to calm the waters by writing a "Preface of the Translators" to explain why the King James Version had been made.

However, most King James Versions being printed today, many decent decades really, though they contain a lengthy dedication to King James, they omit from the usual printings the "Preface of the Translators." If they retained this preface, the modern King James Version reader would have a better understanding of the purpose of the revision. First, the reader would be aware that the King James Version was an improved revision of other earlier English translations. Second, the reader would learn that opposition to a revised translation is to be expected because people are familiar with their current trusted translation that they feel to be the most accurate. Third, the reader would be more receptive to the current translations that they make the exact same argument about say, "we do not want to use your revisions (RV 1881, ASV 1902, RSV 1952, NRSV 1989, NASB 1995, ESV 2001, UASV, 2018), as we have the one true translation that we trust and know."

In part the "Preface of the Translators" says:

> Many mens mouths haue bene open a good while (and yet are not stopped) with speeches about the Translation so long in hand . . . : and aske what may be the reason, what the necessitie of the employment.[79] [Many men's mouths have been open a good while (and yet are not stopped) with speeches about the Translation so long in hand . . . : and asked what may be the reason, what the necessity of the employment.]

Again, the King James Version reader would learn that the *King James Version* was a revision of earlier English Translations made with a modest hope of improvement and they had no thought of finality:

> Truly (good Christian Reader) wee neuer thought from the beginning, that we should neede to make a new Translation, nor yet to make of a bad one a good one, . . . but to make a good one better, or out of many good ones, one principall good one, not justly to be excepted against; that hath bene our indeauour, that our marke.[80] [Truly (good Christian Reader) we never thought from the beginning, that we should need to make a new Translation, nor yet to make of a bad one a good one, . . . but

---

[79] Gordon Campbell, *The Holy Bible: King James Version, Quatercentenary Edition* (Oxford, England, UK: Oxford University Press, 2010), xv.

[80] IBID.

to make a good one better, or out of many good ones, one principal good one, not justly to be excepted against; that has been our endeavor, that our mark.]

In his study on the King James Bible and its tradition, Alister McGrath writes: "A careful study of the way in which the King James Bible translates the Greek and Hebrew originals suggests that the translators felt obliged to: 1) Ensure that every word in the original was rendered by an English equivalent; 2) Make it clear when they added any words to make the sense clearer, or to lead to better English syntax. . . . 3) Follow the basic word order of the original wherever possible."[81]

Bruce M. Metzger writes, "The aim of the revisers is clearly stated in the preface. It was not to make 'a new translation, nor yet to make of a bad one a good one ... but to make a good one better, or out of many good ones one principal good one.' Although usually called a translation,' it is in fact merely a revision of the Bishops' Bible, as this itself was a revision of the Great Bible, and the Great Bible a revision of Coverdale and Tyndale. A great deal of the praise, therefore, that is given to it belongs to its predecessors. For the idiom and vocabulary, Tyndale deserves the greatest credit; for the melody and harmony, Coverdale;5 for scholarship and accuracy, the Geneva version."[82]

Leland Ryken observes, "within a few decades it supplanted the Geneva Bible as the dominant English version. Although the KJV eventually came to be known as the Authorized Version—the AV—it did not, in fact, receive the advantage of being officially sanctioned by either the king or the clerical hierarchy (even though the title page claimed that it was 'appointed to be read in Churches')."[83]

Changes to the King James Version

Today no one reads the *King James Version* in its original form of 1611. Many readers of the King James Version would be quite surprised to know of the many changes to the King James Bible throughout the centuries. There have been so many changes to the King James Version the Committee on Versions (1851-56) of the American Bible Society found 24,000 variations in six different editions of the King James Version! Metzger tells

---

[81] John Beekman and John Callow, *Translating the Word of God* (Grand Rapids, MI: Zondervan, 1974), 25.

[82] Bruce Metzger. Bible in Translation, The: Ancient and English Versions (pp. 76-77).

[83] Ryken, Leland. Understanding English Bible Translation: The Case for an Essentially Literal Approach (Kindle Locations 638-641). Crossway. Kindle Edition.

us that "the first printing of the version, as would be expected, contained some typographic errors-averaging about one in ten pages. In Exodus 14:10, three whole lines were repeated: "the children of Israel lift up their eyes, and beholde, the Egyptians marched after them, and they were sore afraid." A printer's error that has been perpetuated in editions of the KJV to the present time is "strain at a gnat" (Matt. 23:24) instead of "strain out a gnat." Of all the misprints that have disfigured various printings of the version, none has been so scandalous as the omission of the word "not" from the seventh commandment in an edition of 1631, which then read "Thou shalt commit adultery" (Exod. 20:14), for which the king's printers were fined three hundred pounds by Archbishop Laud."[84]

The argument from the King James reader, who refuses to even consider the updated, revised, far more accurate modern translations is that the Bible has been changed and they believe that the King James Version was perfect, some even thinking it was an inspired translation, the very inerrant, authoritative Word of God that has never been changed, error-free. Sadly, for these readers, the King James Version has already been changed many times and has thousands of errors, so their beliefs about the King James Version is extremely mistaken, lying on a crumbled foundation. In addition, why do the modern day King James Version readers not read the 1611 edition? Because the King James Version today, with its many corrections over the centuries is far easier to read. They are unknowingly not aware of the improvements to the King James Version. They would not want to read "fet" for "fetched," "sith" for "since" or "moe" for "more," as the edition of 1611 had it.

If these persons do not want it changed, then why do they use, instead of a copy of an edition of 1611, an edition that has been changed? They use a present-day edition of the King James Bible because it is far easier to read. They appreciate, perhaps unknowingly, the improvements the later editions have made. They do not like the odd spelling and punctuation of the 1611 edition; they do not want to read "fet" for "fetched," "sith" for "since" or "moe" for "more," as the edition of 1611 had it. Thus, improvement, when needed, is unknowingly appreciated, even by those who say they do not want modern translations because they have changed the Bible.

The English of the 1611 era is as such at Roman 6:1-7, "What shall we saye then? Shall we continue in synne that there maye be aboundaunce of grace? God forbyd. How shall we that are deed as touchynge synne live eny lenger therin? Remember ye not that all we which are baptysed in the

---

[84] Bruce Metzger. Bible in Translation, The: Ancient and English Versions (p. 78).

name of Iesu Christ are baptysed to dye with him? We are buryed with him by baptim for to dye that lykewyse as Christ was raysed vp from deeth by the glorye of the father: eve so we also shuld walke in a newe lyfe. For yf we be graft in deeth lyke vnto him: even so must we be in the resurreccio. This we must remeber that oure olde man is crucified with him also that the body of synne myght vtterly be destroyed that hence forth we shuld not be servauntes of synne. For he that is deed ys iustified from synne. Wherfore yf we be deed with Christ we beleve that we shall live with him: 9 remembringe that Christ once raysed fro deeth dyeth no more. Deeth hath no moare power over him."

The vast number of improvements to the King James Version over the centuries is just a fraction of what is needed, which modern literal translations are providing to their readers by keeping pace with changing language. Therefore, they are making God's Word clear, understandable, alive.

The Sixteen Missing Verses Or The Sixteen Added Verses?

This is just some of the lengthier interpolations that the unaware propagate by saying that they are missing. **Interpolation:** the addition of spurious material to the text by a scribe. Philip Comfort glossary reads, "**Interpolation.** inserted new word or words that results in changing the original text."[85] These verses are not missing from the modern translations, they were not in the original text, as they were later additions to the Greek New Testament text by the copyist.

Matthew 17:21 King James Version (KJV)	Matthew 17:21 American Standard Version (ASV), Also ESV, LEB, CSB, UASV, others
²¹ Howbeit this kind goeth not out but by prayer and fasting.	21 _____

Matthew 17:21

The external evidence against including this verse is substantial, including ℵ* B (the two earliest manuscripts), 0281 (a seventh-century manuscript discovered at St. Catherine's Monastery in the late twentieth century), and early witnesses of Old Latin, Coptic, and Syriac. If the verse was originally part of Matthew's gospel, there is no good reason to explain

---

[85] Philip Comfort, *Encountering the Manuscripts: An Introduction to New Testament Paleography & Textual Criticism* (Nashville, TN: Broadman & Holman, 2005), 385.

why it was dropped from so many early and diverse witnesses. Thus, it is far more likely that this added verse was assimilated from Mark 9:29 in its long form, which has the additional words "and fasting." In fact, the same manuscripts (ℵ² C D L W f¹· Maj) that have the long form in Mark 9:29 have the additional verse here. Thus, a scribe took the full verse of Mark 9:29 as presented in his manuscript and inserted it here; most other manuscripts maintained this insertion in the transmission of the text. (The short form in Mark 9:29 appears in ℵ* B.) The verse is included in KJV and NKJV and excluded in all other modern versions except NASB and HCSB which include the verse in brackets.[86]

Matthew 18:11 King James Version (KJV) ¹¹ For the Son of man is come to save that which was lost.	Matthew 8:11 American Standard Version (ASV), Also ESV, LEB, CSB, UASV, others ¹¹ _____

Matthew 18:11

The absence of this verse in several important and diverse witnesses attests to the fact that it was not part of the original text of Matthew. It was borrowed from Luke 19:10, a passage not at all parallel to this one. Most likely the addition first appeared in the shorter form (variant 1), and was later expanded to the longer form (variant 2), which concurs exactly with Luke 19:10. The manuscript L demonstrates all three phases: L* omits the verse; L has the shorter form of the addition, and L has the longer form.

Very likely this verse was inserted in Matt 18 to provide some sort of bridge between verses 10 and 12. In other words, a scribe perceived there was a semantic gap that needed filling. Luke 19:10 was used to introduce the illustration of a shepherd seeking out its lost sheep (the longer form also speaks of "seeking out," which makes the connection even clearer). However, the text must be read without the bridge that 18:11 provides. Verse 12 follows verse 10 in the original in that it provides yet another reason for why the "little ones who believe in Jesus" should not be despised: The shepherd is concerned for each and every sheep in the flock. In a flock of 100 sheep, if even one leaves, he will seek it out and find it.[87]

---

[86] Philip W. Comfort, *New Testament Text and Translation Commentary: Commentary on the Variant Readings of the Ancient New Testament Manuscripts and How They Relate to the Major English Translations* (Carol Stream, IL: Tyndale House Publishers, Inc., 2008), 51.

[87] IBID, 52–53.

Matthew 23:14 King James Version (KJV)	Matthew 23:14 American Standard Version (ASV), Also ESV, LEB, CSB, UASV, others
¹⁴ Woe unto you, scribes and Pharisees, hypocrites! for ye devour widows' houses, and for a pretence make long prayer: therefore ye shall receive the greater damnation.	14 ———

Matthew 23:14

This verse, not present in the earliest manuscripts and several other witnesses, was taken from Mark 12:40 or Luke 20:47 and inserted in later manuscripts either before or after 23:13. This kind of gospel harmonization became especially prevalent after the fourth century. It is noteworthy that KJV and NKJV did not follow TR in placing the verse before verse 13, but after it. The verse is noted in modern versions out of deference for its place in English Bible history. Undoubtedly, the HCSB includes the verse out of deference to its KJV- and NKJV-friendly readership, but this does not help these readers understand that KJV is based on inferior manuscript support.[88]

Mark 7:16 King James Version (KJV)	Mark 7:16 American Standard Version (ASV), Also ESV, LEB, CSB, UASV, others
¹⁶ If any man have ears to hear, let him hear.	16 ———

Mark 7:16

The WH NU reading has the earliest support among the manuscripts. The extra verse was added by scribes, borrowing it directly from 4:23 (see also 4:9) to provide an ending to an otherwise very short pericope, 7:14–15. This addition was included in TR and made popular by KJV, NKJV, NASB, NJB, and HCSB also include this extra verse.[89]

Mark 9:44 & 9:46 King James Version (KJV)	Mark 9:44 & 9:46 American Standard Version (ASV)), Also ESV, LEB, CSB, UASV, others
⁴⁴ Where their worm dieth not, and the fire is not quenched.	44, 46 ———

---

[88] IBID, 69–70.

[89] IBID, 121.

| ⁴⁶ Where their worm dieth not, and the fire is not quenched. | |

Mark 9:44, 46

Although it could be argued that these verses were omitted by scribes who considered the repetition to be unnecessary, such a deletion could hardly occur in manuscripts of such vast diversity as those that give witness to the absence of these verses. Contrarily, verses 44 and 46 were added as a sort of prophetic refrain that makes for good oral reading. Indeed, many textual variants entered the textual stream as the result of scribes enhancing the text for oral reading in the church. This is a classic example. Several modern English versions omit these verses and then note their inclusion for the sake of readers familiar with their place in the KJV tradition. By retaining the verses in the text, the HCSB retains the KJV tradition.[90]

Mark 11:26 King James Version (KJV)	Mark 11:26 American Standard Version (ASV), Also ESV, LEB, CSB, UASV, others
²⁶ But if ye do not forgive, neither will your Father which is in heaven forgive your trespasses.	26 ⎯⎯⎯

Mark 11:26

Though it could be argued that verse 26 dropped out by a scribal mistake (both 11:25 and 11:26 end with the same three words), the WH NU reading has much better documentation than the variant. Thus, it is more likely that verse 26 is a natural scribal expansion of verse 25, borrowed from Matt 6:15, a parallel verse (cf. Matt 18:35). According to Mark's original text, Jesus was encouraging people to forgive others their trespasses against them before seeking forgiveness from God for their own trespasses. The addition makes God's forgiveness conditional. The extra verse is included in TR, followed by KJV, NKJV, as well as by NASB and HCSB, which persist in maintaining the KJV tradition. It is noted in modern versions out of deference to the KJV tradition.[91]

Mark 15:28 King James Version (KJV)	Mark 15:28 American Standard Version (ASV), Also ESV, LEB, CSB, UASV, others
²⁸ And the scripture was fulfilled, which saith, And he was numbered with the transgressors.	28 ⎯⎯⎯

---

[90] IBID, 133.

[91] IBID, 142.

Mark 15:28

The documentary evidence decisively shows that this verse was not present in any Greek manuscript prior to the late sixth century (namely, 083—a manuscript discovered in the 1970s at St. Catherine's Monastery). Borrowing from a parallel passage, Luke 22:37 (which is a quotation of Isa 53:12), later scribes inserted this verse as a prophetic proof text for the phenomenon of Jesus' death with the lawless. Of all the gospel writers, Mark was by far the least concerned with showing prophetic fulfillment in the events of Jesus' life. No doubt, his Roman audience (hardly aware of the OT Scriptures) influenced this literary approach. In any event, the verse is retained in KJV and NKJV, as well as in NASB and HCSB, which usually follow KJV with respect to keeping verses in the text—in contrast to all other modern versions.[92]

Luke 17:36 King James Version (KJV)	Luke 17:36 American Standard Version (ASV), Also ESV, LEB, CSB, UASV, others
36 Two men shall be in the field; the one shall be taken, and the other left.	36 ――

Luke 17:36

Although it is possible that the verse could have been omitted due to homoeoteleuton, it is hardly possible that the mistake would have occurred in so many manuscripts of such great diversity. Therefore, it is far more likely that the verse is a scribal interpolation borrowed from Matt 24:40, with harmonization to the style of Luke 17:35. Though the verse is not present in TR, it was included in KJV (perhaps under the influence of the Latin Vulgate), NKJV, and HCSB, which in deference to KJV has a pattern of including verses that are omitted by all other modern versions.[93]

John 5:3–4 King James Version (KJV)	John 5:3–4 American Standard Version (ASV), Also ESV, LEB, CSB, UASV, others
3 In these lay a great multitude of impotent folk, of blind, halt, withered, waiting for the moving of the water.	3 In these lay a multitude of them that were sick, blind, halt, withered ―― 4 ――

---

[92] IBID, 154.

[93] IBID, 221.

⁴ For an angel went down at a certain season into the pool, and troubled the water: whosoever then first after the troubling of the water stepped in was made whole of whatsoever disease he had.

John 5:3b–4

This portion (5:3b–4) was probably not written by John, because it is not found in the earliest manuscripts (𝔓⁶⁶ 𝔓⁷⁵ ℵ B C* T), and where it does occur in later manuscripts it is often marked with obeli (marks like asterisks) to signal spuriousness (so Π 047 syr^h marking 5:4). The passage was a later addition—even added to manuscripts, such as A and C, that did not originally contain the portion. This scribal gloss is characteristic of the expansions that occurred in gospel texts after the fourth century. The expansion happened in two phases: First came the addition of 5:3b—inserted to explain what the sick people were waiting for; and then came 5:4—inserted to provide an explanation about the troubling of the water mentioned in 5:7. Of course, the second expansion is fuller and more imaginative. Nearly all modern textual critics and translators will not accept the longer portion as part of the original text. NASB and HCSB, however, continue to retain verses in deference to the KJV tradition.[94]

Acts 8:37 King James Version (KJV)	Acts 8:37 American Standard Version (ASV), Also ESV, LEB, CSB, UASV, others
³⁷ And Philip said, If thou believest with all thine heart, thou mayest. And he answered and said, I believe that Jesus Christ is the Son of God.	³⁷ ———

Acts 8:37

If the verse was an original part of Luke's text, there is no good reason for explaining why it would have been omitted in so many ancient manuscripts and versions. Rather, this verse is a classic example of scribal gap-filling, in that it supplied the apparent gap left by the unanswered question of the previous verse ("The eunuch said, 'Look, here is water! What is to prevent me from being baptized?' "). The interpolation puts an answer on Philip's lips that is derived from ancient Christian baptismal practices. Before being baptized, the new believer had to make a confession

---

[94] IBID, 272–273.

of his or her faith in Jesus as the Son of God. A similar addition also worked its way into the text of John 9:38-39 (see note).

There is nothing doctrinally wrong with this interpolation; it affirms belief with the heart (in accordance with verses like Rom 10:9-10) and elicits the response of faith in Jesus Christ as the Son of God (in accordance with verses like John 20:31). But it is not essential that one make such a verbatim confession before being baptized. In fact, the eunuch had made no such confession, but it was obvious to Philip that he believed Jesus was the Messiah when the eunuch said, "Look, here is water. What prevents me from being baptized?" This is part of the beauty of the book of Acts: Many individuals come to faith in Christ in a variety of ways. The church throughout history has had a habit of standardizing the way people express their faith in Christ.

It is difficult to know when this interpolation first entered the text, but it could have been as early as the second century since Irenaeus (*Haer.* 3.12.8) quoted part of it. The earliest extant Greek manuscript to include it is E, of the sixth century. Erasmus included the verse in his edition of the Greek New Testament because—even though it was not present in many of the manuscripts he knew—he considered it to have been omitted by the carelessness of scribes. He based its inclusion on a marginal reading in codex 4 (see TCGNT). From Erasmus's edition, it worked its way into TR and subsequently KJV. The only reason it is printed in the margins of all the other versions is that translations invariably inform the reader about instances in which the text omits a verse that is often included in other prominent versions, especially KJV. The NASB and HCSB, with typical sensitivity to the KJV tradition, include the verse, though it is set in brackets.[95]

| **Acts 15:34** King James Version (KJV)

34 Notwithstanding it pleased Silas to abide there still. | **Acts 15:34** American Standard Version (ASV), Also ESV, LEB, CSB, UASV, others

34 _____ |

Acts 15:34

The extra verse, though it contradicts 15:33, was added to avoid the difficulty in 15:40, which indicates that Silas was still in Antioch. Thus, in trying to solve one problem, the reviser (and other scribes) created another.

We may wonder how a verse that was not included in the Byzantine text (Maj) was incorporated into TR. The verse (in form 1) was inserted by Erasmus into his Greek text, even though he found it only in the margin of

---

[95] IBID, 363-364.

the Greek manuscripts he was using. Erasmus, probably aware of its inclusion in the Latin Vulgate, supposed that it had been omitted in the Greek manuscripts by an error of the scribes (Westcott and Hort 1882, 96). From Erasmus's text it went into TR and was then translated in KJV. Most modern versions note the omission out of deference to the KJV tradition. NASB retains the verse with a note saying that early manuscripts do not contain it.[96]

Acts 24:6–8 King James Version (KJV)	Acts 24:6–8 American Standard Version (ASV), Also ESV, LEB, CSB, UASV, others
⁶ Who also hath gone about to profane the temple: whom we took, and would have judged according to our law. ⁷ But the chief captain Lysias came upon us, and with great violence took him away out of our hands, ⁸ Commanding his accusers to come unto thee: by examining of whom thyself mayest take knowledge of all these things, whereof we accuse him.	⁶ who moreover assayed to profane the temple: on whom also we laid hold: —— ⁸ from whom thou wilt be able, by examining him thyself, to take knowledge of all these things whereof we accuse him.

Acts 24:6–8

The expanded reading, found primarily in Western manuscripts, produces a rendering of these verses in TR such as this: "⁶ He even tried to profane the temple, and so we seized him. And we would have judged him according to our law. ⁷ But the chief captain Lysias came and with great violence took him out of our hands, ⁸ commanding his accusers to come before you. By examining him yourself you will be able to learn from him concerning everything of which we accuse him."

The variant reading, which found its way into the majority of manuscripts and was included in TR, is another example of gap-filling. The words are included, of course, by KJV and NKJV as well as NASB and HCSB, which often include verses that all other modern translations exclude. The words were added because a scribe did not think it likely that Felix would have received the whole story from Paul. Therefore, he connected the relative pronoun in the phrase παρ ου ("from whom") to Lysias, the tribune

---

[96] IBID, 393–394.

who rescued Paul from the Jews plotting to kill him. The same idea of using military power or force (μετα πολλης βιας) to accomplish this rescue is found in the Western addition to 23:29 (see note). But Lysias was not present to give Felix an account of these things, so the expanded variant is wrong. The text, without the interpolation, is bare but understandable: Paul was arrested so that he could now be examined and tried by Felix.[97]

Acts 28:29 King James Version (KJV)	Acts 28:29 American Standard Version (ASV), Also ESV, LEB, CSB, UASV, others
29 And when he had said these words, the Jews departed, and had great reasoning among themselves.	29 _____

Acts 28:29

The additional verse passed from the Western text into the Byzantine text. It was added to fill in the narrative gap between 28:28 and 28:30. All modern versions except NASB and HCSB do not include it in the text. Most note it out of deference to the KJV tradition.[98]

Romans 16:24 King James Version (KJV)	Romans 16:24 American Standard Version (ASV), Also ESV, LEB, CSB, UASV, others
24 The grace of our Lord Jesus Christ be with you all. Amen.	24 _____

Romans 16:24

The omission of this verse is strongly supported by all the earliest manuscripts. The verse was copied from 16:20 by some scribe (or scribes) who thought it was also suited to follow the postscript (see note on 16:20). Since TR and Majority Text include this verse, so do KJV and NKJV. The Western manuscripts (D F G) add the benediction at 16:24 because they do not include 16:25–27. All modern translations, following superior testimony, do not include the verse. At the same time, these translations provide a textual note concerning this verse because of its place in traditional English translations. The textual situation of 16:24 must be considered along with 16:25–27 (see following note).[99]

---

[97] IBID, 423–424.

[98] IBID, 433.

[99] IBID, 477.

1 John 5:7-8 King James Version (KJV, ASV)	1 John 5:7-8 Updated American Standard Version (UASV), Also ESV, LEB, CSB, others
⁷ For there are three that bear record in heaven, the Father, the Word, and the Holy Ghost: and these three are one. ⁸ And there are three that bear witness in earth, the Spirit, and the water, and the blood: and these three agree in one.	⁷ For there are three that testify: ⁸ ——

1 John 5:7b–8

John never wrote the following words: "in heaven, the Father, the Word, and the Holy Spirit: and these three are one. And there are three that bear witness in earth." This famous passage, called "the heavenly witness" or *Comma Johanneum*, came from a gloss on 5:8 which explained that the three elements (water, blood, and Spirit) symbolize the Trinity (the Father, the Word [Son], and the Spirit).

This gloss had a Latin origin (as did the one in 5:20—see note). The first time this passage appears in the longer form (with the heavenly witness) is in the treatise *Liber Apologeticus*, written by the Spanish heretic Priscillian (died ca. 385) or his follower, Bishop Instantius. Metzger said, "apparently the gloss arose when the original passage was understood to symbolize the Trinity (through the mention of the three witnesses: the Spirit, the water, and the blood), an interpretation which may have been written first as a marginal note that afterward found its way into the text" (TCGNT). The gloss showed up in the writings of Latin fathers in North Africa and Italy (as part of the text of the Epistle) from the fifth century onward, and it found its way into more and more copies of the Latin Vulgate. (The original translation of Jerome did not include it.) "The heavenly witnesses" passage has not been found in the text of any Greek manuscript prior to the fourteenth century, and it was never cited by any Greek father. Many of the Greek manuscripts listed above (in support of the variant reading) do not even include the extra verbiage in the text but rather record these words as a "variant reading" (v.r.) in the margin.

Erasmus did not include "the heavenly witnesses" passage in the first two editions of his Greek New Testament. He was criticized for this by defenders of the Latin Vulgate. Erasmus, in reply, said that he would include it if he could see it in any one Greek manuscript. In turn, a manuscript (most likely the Monfort Manuscript, 61, of the sixteenth century) was specially fabricated to contain the passage and thereby fool Erasmus. Erasmus kept his promise; he included it in the third edition. From there it became incorporated into TR and was translated in the KJV. Both KJV and NKJV have popularized this expanded passage. The NKJV translators included it in the text, knowing full well that it has no place there. This is evident in their footnote: "Only four or five very late manuscripts contain these words in Greek." Its inclusion in the text demonstrates their commitment to maintaining the KJV heritage.

Without the intrusive words, the text reads: "For there are three that testify: the Spirit, the water, and the blood; and the three are in agreement" (NIV). It has nothing to do with the Triune God, but with the three critical phases in Jesus' life where he was manifested as God incarnate, the Son of God in human form. This was made evident at his baptism (= the water), his death (= the blood), and his resurrection (= the Spirit). At his baptism, the man Jesus was declared God's beloved Son (see Matt 3:16–17). At his crucifixion, a man spilling blood was recognized by others as "God's Son" (see Mark 15:39). In the resurrection, he was designated as the Son of God in power (see Rom 1:3–4). This threefold testimony is unified in one aspect: Each event demonstrated that the man Jesus was the divine Son of God.[100]

Chapter 8 is going to give the reader even more insights into the King James Version that in all likelihood, they were not aware of but should know for salvation depends upon it.

---

[100] IBID, 784–785.

CHAPTER 8 KING JAMES VERSION
Read the Bible to Understand It

Above All Acquire Wisdom

Proverbs 4:7 Updated American Standard Version (UASV)

⁷ The beginning of wisdom is this: Acquire wisdom,
and with all you acquire, acquire understanding.

The beginning of wisdom is this: Acquire wisdom: Here the Hebrew has two detached phrases that are literally "the first thing of wisdom" and "get wisdom." Here King David in his advice to his son when Solomon was young was that wisdom is the most important thing, and therefore, he should pursue it so as to obtain it.

Wisdom: (Heb. *ḥāḵ·mā(h)*) is sound judgment, based on knowledge and understanding. It is the balanced application of that knowledge to answer difficulties, achieve objectives, sidestep or ward off dangers, not to mention helping others to accomplish the same. The wise person is often contrasted with the foolishness or stupid person. – Deut. 32:6; Prov. 11:29; Eccles. 6:8.

And with all you acquire, acquire understanding is again places the highest importance on obtaining or acquiring but this time it is in the pursuit of understanding or insight.

Understanding (Heb. *tᵉḇû·nā(h)*) is the ability to see how the parts or aspects of something are connected to one another. One who possesses understanding can see the big picture (the entire matter) and not just the isolated facts. – Prov. 2:5; 9:10; 18:15.

Insight (Heb. *bî·nā(h)*) is the ability to see into a situation. One who possesses insight acts with wisdom, caution, and discretion. Insight is closely related to understanding, but there is a fine distinction between the two terms. Says the *Theological Wordbook of the Old Testament:* "While *bîn* [understanding] indicates "distinguishing between," *śākal* relates to an intelligent knowledge of the reason. There is the process of thinking through a complex arrangement of thoughts resulting in a wise dealing and use of good practical common sense. Another end result is the emphasis upon being successful."[101] – Psa. 14:12.

As we learned in Proverbs chapter three, wisdom is the ability to apply knowledge and understanding effectively, to have success. Knowledge is acquired by our taking in facts that were gained by paying attention and experience, as well as through reading and study. However, all of that is useless if one cannot put that information to work for them. Insight is the ability to see into a situation. When one acts with insight, he has good sense in dealing with practical matters, using good judgment to consider likely consequences and act accordingly, as well as discretion. We are foolish if we forsake wisdom, as she will protect us from the difficulties of this system of things, but that protection only comes to those that remain loyal in our love for her. If we lack wisdom, then we must begin to pursue it, in addition to insight.

The education of an Israelite child was taken very seriously, as Jehovah himself commanded that parent, "You shall teach them [the law] diligently to your sons and shall talk of them when you sit in your house and when you walk by the way and when you lie down and when you rise up." (Deut. 6:7) However, before they were to teach their child, it was commanded: "these words, which I am commanding you today, shall be on your heart." (Deut. 6:6) As Deuteronomy, 6:7 made quite clear there is no excuse for not spending time with your child and passing on wisdom and insight is paramount.

Acquire wisdom, and with all you acquire, acquire understanding. commands King David to his young son Solomon. How can you apply this counsel to our Bible reading? The Bible of sixty-six books is the only book to be authored by God as he used 40+ men, moving them along with the Holy Spirit as they wrote. The Bible contains God's thoughts. There is more to acquiring God's thoughts than merely reading the printed words on a page. We must understand what we read. Moreover, we must understand what the author meant by the words that were used, as opposed to interjecting what we feel, think, or believe God meant by those words. So, we need to meditatively read, study, and research the Bible, then, acquiring an understanding of what God meant to convey to us by the words of wisdom that he used.

One way that we can know whether we are reading, studying, and researching the Bible to understand the words of wisdom correctly is to ask

---

[101] R. Laird Harris, Gleason L. Archer Jr., and Bruce K. Waltke, eds., *Theological Wordbook of the Old Testament* (Chicago: Moody Press, 1999), 877.

ourselves what translation of the Bible are we using and why are we using this particular Bible? Are we using it because it is an easy to understand translation (CEV, GNT, NLT, NIV, etc.)? Or, are we using it because it is familiar to us and we are accustomed to using it (KJV)? Or are we using it because we know it is accurate and faithful to the original text and it is going to give us what God said by way of his human authors, not what a translator thinks God meant in its place? (ASV, RSV, NASB, CSB, NASB, and especially the UASV)[102] In chapters 5-7, we already discussed using the dynamic equivalent, interpretive, easy to understand translations.

In chapter 8, we had earnestly begun the discussion of using the King James Version. Here we continue with the most widely used English translation of the Bible, the King James Version, which most readers use because are familiar with it and unfamiliar with modern translations, mainly because they refuse to give modern translations a hearing ear. Some prefer the beautiful Shakespearean language, possibly, and do not want to see it changed. In many cases, they are unknowingly reading the Bible more for its literary effect than for understanding. Or, they have mistakenly thought that the King James Version is itself inspired by God, unchanged, error-free, and authorized. In the previous chapter, Do You Really Know the King James Version, we learned that there is no sound basis for any Christian to believe that the King James Version is itself inspired by God, unchanged, error-free, and authorized.

Considering that the Bible was written originally in written Hebrew, Aramaic, and Greek; then, translation into today's modern languages is necessary. Thus, we have seen in the past few decades many modern translations of the Bible, with there now being over 100 English translations alone. Here again, the most used English Bible being the King James Version was published over four hundred years ago in 1611, which makes it the most dated (out of date, archaic) translation that we have. In 1611, the language was modern and up to date. However, language changes in decades, let alone centuries. As a result, the readers of the King James Version believe that they know and understand what they are reading but they are really failing to understand it fully. This is very serious. These devoted Christians have exhibited a willful blindness to the truth about translation.

Language Changes Obscure Understanding

As we have noted hundreds of years have passed since the days of King James hundreds of English words have changed in meaning or have

---

[102] https://www.uasvbible.org/

taken on new meanings, even the opposite of what was meant in 1611. When these modern-day readers of the King James Version come across these words, they obscure their understanding of what the author meant, while the reader of four hundred years ago readily understood them the right way. How sad that these changes in the meaning of words have unknowingly caused confusion and blocked understanding to a people so dedicated to the Word of God.

Conversation

1 Peter 3:1-2 King James Version (KJV)	1 Peter 3:1-2 English Standard Version (ESV)	1 Peter 3:1-2 New American Standard Bible (NASB)	1 Peter 3:1-2 Updated American Standard Version (UASV)
3 Likewise, ye wives, be in subjection to your own husbands; that, if any obey not the word, they also may without the word be won by the **conversation** of the wives; ² While they behold your **chaste conversation** coupled with fear.	**3** Likewise, wives, be subject to your own husbands, so that even if some do not obey the word, they may be won without a word by the **conduct** of their wives, ² when they see your **respectful and pure conduct**.	**3** In the same way, you wives, be submissive to your own husbands so that even if any *of them* are disobedient to the word, they may be won without a word by the **behavior** of their wives, ² as they observe your **chaste and respectful behavior**.	**3** In the same way, you wives, be submissive to your own husbands so that even if any of them are disobedient to the word, they may be won without a word by the **behavior** of their wives, ² as they observe your **chaste and respectful behavior**.

Today, the word **conversation** is the informal exchange of ideas by spoken words. Consequently, how are modern readers of the King James Version to understand the apostle Paul's counsel to Christian wives that unbelieving husbands may be won over to the faith "**by the conversation of the wives; While they behold your chaste conversation** coupled with fear." Now, what does that even mean, really? Does it mean that Christian

108

wives can win over their unbelieving husbands through conversation, the exchange of ideas? And must a Christian wife **fear** her husband?

Now, the King James Version reader believe that they know what the word **conversation** and the word **fear** mean so they come away with the wrong understanding of what Paul meant by the Greek words that he used. Why can we say this with certainty? Because the word conversation meant something completely different four hundred years ago. In 1611, the word conversation meant, "General course of manners; behavior; deportment; especially as it respects morals."[103] Now that we have a better understanding of the koine (common) Greek of the first century, we know the Greek noun (*anastrophē*) means "**behavior**, way of life, one's conduct in life (Gal 1:13; Eph 4:22; Heb 13:7; 1Pe 1:15; 3:1; 2Pe 3:11)"[104] Yes, the meaning is of a person's moral conduct or behavior, which means that an unbelieving husband can "be won without a word by the **behavior** of their wives."

In addition, the husband is not won over by the **fear** of the wife but rather as the Greek noun (*phobos*) says, profound respect or chaste respect. Yes, it is true that the primary meaning of *phobos* is **fear**. However, as we all know today, Greek is like all other languages and ever word has several different meanings. "**phobos**; from **φέβομαι phebomai** *(to be put to flight); panic flight, fear, the causing of fear, terror.* – cause of fear (1), fear (37), fearful (1), fears (1), intimidation (1), respect (1), respectful (1), reverence (1), sense of awe (1)."[105] A modern-day English example would be the word hand, it has 24 different meanings, such as the end part of a person's arm beyond the wrist, but also the hand on a clock, a hand of cards, the hand (worker) on an oil rig, and many more. The meaning is according to the context. If the context was the **hand** of God, the meaning would be the power of God, another one of the twenty-four different meanings.

---

[103] KJV Dictionary (Thursday, August 9, 2018) https://av1611.com/kjbp/kjv-dictionary/

[104] James Swanson, *Dictionary of Biblical Languages with Semantic Domains: Greek (New Testament)* (Oak Harbor: Logos Research Systems, Inc., 1997).

[105] Robert L. Thomas, *New American Standard Hebrew-Aramaic and Greek Dictionaries: Updated Edition* (Anaheim: Foundation Publications, Inc., 1998).

Shambles

1 Corinthians 10:24-25 King James Version (KJV)	1 Corinthians 10:24-25 English Standard Version (ESV)	1 Corinthians 10:24-25 New American Standard Bible (NASB)	1 Corinthians 10:24-25 Updated American Standard Version (UASV)
24 Let no man seek his own, but **every man** another's **wealth**. 25 Whatsoever is sold in the **shambles**, that eat, asking no question for conscience sake:	24 Let no one seek his own good, but **the good of his neighbor**. 25 Eat whatever is sold in the **meat market** without raising any question on the ground of conscience.	24 Let no one **seek** his own *good*, but that **of his neighbor**. 25 Eat anything that is sold in the **meat market** without asking questions for conscience' sake;	24 Let each one **keep seeking**, not his own **good**, but that **of the other person**. 25 Eat whatever is sold in the **meat market** without raising questions for the sake of conscience.

The King James Version reader is likely wondering what did Paul mean by **seeking another man's wealth**? Moreover, what is **shambles**? What kind of food might one buy at a shambles? In 1611, shambles meant "The place where butcher's meat is sold; a meat market." Yes, the Greek noun (*makellon*) means "**meat market**, food market (1Co 10:25+)."[106] How much clearer the understanding is now. Of course, the King James Version preacher has likely been giving the modern-day reader the meaning of shambles by saying, *shambles or meat market*, as he gives his sermon. Yet, this does not take away that there are over one thousand words in the King James Version that do not mean today what they meant in 1611. For goodness sake, they have a King James Version dictionary. (av1611.com) Lastly, on this verse, we do not seek another man's wealth but rather we keep seeking the good of the other person.

---

[106] James Swanson, *Dictionary of Biblical Languages with Semantic Domains: Greek (New Testament)* (Oak Harbor: Logos Research Systems, Inc., 1997).

Addicted

1 Corinthians 16:15 King James Version (KJV)	1 Corinthians 16:15 English Standard Version (ESV)	1 Corinthians 16:15 New American Standard Bible (NASB)	1 Corinthians 16:15 Updated American Standard Version (UASV)
¹⁵ I beseech you, brethren, (ye know the house of Stephanas, that it is the firstfruits of Achaia, and that they have **addicted** themselves to the ministry of the saints,)	¹⁵ Now I urge you, brothers—you know that the household of Stephanas were the first converts in Achaia, and that they have **devoted** themselves to the service of the saints	¹⁵ Now I urge you, brethren (you know the household of Stephanas, that they were the first fruits of Achaia, and that they have **devoted** themselves for ministry to the saints),	¹⁵ Now I urge you, brothers, you know that the household of Stephanas were the first converts in Achaia, and that they have **devoted** themselves to ministering to the holy ones,

Addicted today means *to be physically and mentally dependent* on a particular substance, and unable to stop taking it without incurring adverse effects. However, four hundred years ago, addicted meant *devoted by customary practice*. The Greek verb (*tassō*) means "**give oneself to**, do with devotion (1Co 16:15+)."[107] Yes, the household of Stephanas "**devoted** themselves to ministering to the holy ones," as opposed to the modern understanding of '**addicting** themselves to the ministry of the saints.' Below we have borrowed some entries from the King James Version Bible to move along faster, briefer, so you can see the impact in greater detail. Remember, this is but a handful of words out of more than a thousand.

Sottish Children

Sottish, a word used at Jeremiah 4:22, meaning foolish or stupid children.

---

[107] James Swanson, *Dictionary of Biblical Languages with Semantic Domains: Greek (New Testament)* (Oak Harbor: Logos Research Systems, Inc., 1997).

Overcharge

Overcharge, a word used at 2 Corinthians 2:5, meaning not to say too much, not to exaggerate, not to put it too severely, not to be too harsh.

shall not prevent them

Shall not prevent them, at 1 Thessalonians 4:15 means will not precede those

Space does not allow further discussion of how language in the *King James Version* blocks understanding, but here is a list of a few more examples, together with the word or phrase used by modern translations to enable us to get the meaning that God wanted us to get.

KING JAMES VERSION	ASV, RSV, NRSV, ESV, CSB, UASV, others	BIBLE TEXT
alleging	proving	Acts 17:3
anon	Immediately, at once	Mark 1:30
barbarous	Natives, local people, foreign-speaking people	Acts 28:2
charger	platter	Matthew 14:11
charity	love	1 Corinthians 13:13
cheek teeth	fangs	Joel 1:6
confectionaries	perfume makers, perfumers	1 Samuel 8:13
divers places	various places	Matthew 24:7
drunken	is drunk	1 Corinthians 11:21
leasing	lies	Psalm 4:2
mortify	put to death	Romans 8:13
outlandish women	foreign women	Nehemiah 13:26
publican	tax collector	Matthew 10:3
sons of Belial	Worthless, (lit. *sons of Belial*)	1 Samuel 2:12
sod pottage	was cooking, cooked	Genesis 25:29
suffer	let, permit	Mark 10:14

take no thought	do not be anxious	Matthew 10:19
turtle	turtledove	Song of Solomon 2:12
unicorn	wild ox	Numbers 23:22
winked at	overlooked	Acts 17:30
do you to wit	make known	2 Corinthians 8:1
wotteth not	does not know	Genesis 39:8

Correctly understanding God's Word is the thing of the highest importance. Using the King James Version for a long time, being familiar with the King James Version, family tradition, sentimentality, should not overshadow the importance of understanding what the author meant by the words that were used. As God instructed King David, who counseled young Solomon and by extension us, **with all you acquire, acquire understanding**, which places the highest importance on obtaining or acquiring in our pursuit of understanding or having insight into God's Word.

Many of you readers have been using only the *King James Version* of the Bible. The wise course here is to **acquire** a translation that will bring the meaning of God's Word to you in the most understandable form. We recommend that you Investigate the English Standard Version (ESV), the Lexham English Bible (LEB), the Christian Standard Bible (CSB), the New American Standard Bible (NASB) while you await the full release of the Updated American Standard Version (UASV) – www.uasvbible.org/.

Chapter 9 will not get into the development of the master texts (critical texts) that developed after the Textus Receptus.

CHAPTER 9 The Arrival of the Critical Text Behind Our Modern-Day Bible Translations

New Testament textual criticism goes back to Origen (185-254), in the third century of our common era. The historical roots of textual scholarship actually reach back to the 3rd-century B.C.E. in the Library of Alexandria. We are going to the 18th-19th centuries for the purposes of this chapter.

From 1550, the New Testament Greek text was in bondage to the popularity of the Textus Receptus as though the latter were inspired itself, and no textual scholar would dare make changes regardless of the evidence found in older, more accurate manuscripts that later became known. The best textual scholars would offer was to publish these new findings in the introductions, margins, and footnotes of their editions. Bengel, as we noted above, apologized for repeating the printing of the Textus Receptus "because he could not publish a text of his own. Neither the publisher nor the public would have stood for it." (Robertson 1925, 25)

Karl Lachmann (1793-1851), Professor of Classical and German Philology at Berlin, was the first to make a clean break with the influential Textus Receptus. In 1831, he published at Berlin his edition of the Greek text overthrowing the Textus Receptus. Ezra Abbot says of Lachmann, "He was the first to found a text wholly on ancient evidence; and his editions, to which his eminent reputation as a critic gave wide currency, especially in Germany, did much toward breaking down the superstitious reverence for the textus receptus." (Schaff, Companion to the Greek Testament, 1883, 256-7)

Johann Jakob Griesbach [1745-1812]

Griesbach obtained his master's degree at the age of 23. He was educated at Frankfurt, and at the universities of Tubingen, Leipzig, and Halle. Griesbach became one of Johann Salomo Semler's most dedicated and passionate students. It was Semler (1725 – 1791) who persuaded him to focus his attention on New Testament textual criticism. Even though it was Semler who introduced Griesbach to the theory of text-types, Griesbach is principally responsible for the text-types that we have today. Griesbach made the Alexandrian, Byzantine, and Western text-types appreciated by a wide range of textual scholars over two centuries.

After his master's degree, Griesbach traveled throughout Europe examining Greek manuscripts: Germany, the Netherlands, France, and England. Griesbach would excel far beyond any textual scholar who had preceded him, publishing his Greek text first at Halle in 1775-77, followed by London in 1795-1806, and finally in Leipzig in 1803-07. It would be his latter editions that would be used by a number of Bible translators, such as Archbishop Newcome, Abner Kneeland, Samuel Sharpe, Edgar Taylor, and Benjamin Wilson.

Griesbach was the first to include manuscript readings that were earlier than what Erasmus had used in his Greek text of 1516 C.E. The Society for New Testament Studies comments on the importance of his research: "Griesbach spent long hours in the attempt to find the best readings among the many variants in the New Testament. His work laid the foundations of modern text criticism, and he is, in no small measure, responsible for the secure New Testament text which we enjoy today. Many of his methodological principles continue to be useful in the process of determining the best readings from among the many variants which remain." (B. Orchard 1776-1976, 2005, xi)

The Fifteen Rules of Griesbach

In the Introduction to his Second edition of the **Greek New Testament** (Halle, 1796) **Griesbach** set forth the following list of critical rules for weighing the internal evidence for variant readings within the manuscripts.

1. **The shorter reading is to be preferred over the more verbose**, if not wholly lacking the support of old and weighty witnesses,

for scribes were much more prone to add than to omit. They hardly ever leave out anything on purpose, but they added much. It is true indeed that some things fell out by accident; but likewise not a few things, allowed in by the scribes through errors of the eye, ear, memory, imagination, and judgment, have been added to the text.

The shorter reading is especially preferable (even if by the support of the witnesses it may be second best),

(a) if at the same time it is harder, more obscure, ambiguous, involves an ellipsis, reflects Hebrew idiom, or is ungrammatical;

(b) if the same thing is read expressed with different phrases in different manuscripts;

(c) if the order of words is inconsistent and unstable;

(d) at the beginning of a section;

(e) if the fuller reading gives the impression of incorporating a definition or interpretation, or verbally conforms to parallel passages, or seems to have come in from lectionaries.

But on the contrary, we should set the fuller reading before the shorter (unless the latter is seen in many notable witnesses),

(a) if a "similarity of ending" might have provided an opportunity for an omission;

(b) if that which was omitted could to the scribe have seemed obscure, harsh, superfluous, unusual, paradoxical, offensive to pious ears, erroneous, or opposed to parallel passages;

(c) if that which is absent could be absent without harm to the sense or structure of the words, as for example prepositions which may be called incidental, especially brief ones, and so forth, the lack of which would not easily be noticed by a scribe in reading again what he had written;

(d) if the shorter reading is by nature less characteristic of the style or outlook of the author;

(e) if it wholly lacks sense;

(f) if it is probable that it has crept in from parallel passages or from the lectionaries.

On Griesbach's principle of preferring the shorter reading, James Royse offers a word about appreciating the complexity and exceptions to the rule: "I would certainly accept Silva's reminder that Griesbach's formulation of the *lectio brevior potior* principle is far from a simple preference for the shorter reading, and that its correct application requires a sensitivity to the many exceptions and conditions that Griesbach notes." (J. R. Royse 2007, 735) Kurt and Barbara Aland qualify the principle as well: "The venerable maxim lectio brevior lectio potior ("the shorter reading is the more probable reading") is certainly right in many instances. But here again the principle cannot be applied mechanically. It is not valid for witnesses whose texts otherwise vary significantly from the characteristic patterns of the textual tradition, with frequent omissions or expansions reflecting editorial tendencies (e.g. D)." (Aland and Aland 1995, 281) Harold Greenlee offers a simple (or perhaps simplistic), balanced view of the principle:

(b) The *shorter* reading is generally preferable if an *intentional change* has been made. The reason is that scribes at times made intentional additions to clarify a passage, but rarely made an intentional omission. Of course, this principle applies only to a difference in the number of words in the reading, not to the difference between a longer and a shorter word.

(c) The *longer* reading is often preferable if an *unintentional change* has been made. The reason is that scribes were more likely to omit a word or a phrase accidentally than to add accidentally. (Greenlee, Introduction to New Testament Textual Criticism 1995, 112)

Of Griesbach, Paul D. Wegner writes, "While Griesbach sometimes would rely too heavily on a mechanical adherence to his system of recensions, by and large he was a careful and cautious scholar. He was also the first German scholar to abandon the Textus Receptus in favor of what he believed to be, by means of his principles, superior readings." (Wegner, A Student's Guide to Textual Criticism of the Bible: Its History Methods & Results 2006, 214)

His choosing the shorter reading of the Lord's Prayer at Luke 11:3-4 evidences Griesbach's ability as a textual scholar. He made this decision based on only a handful of minuscule and uncials, patristic, and versional evidence. A few short years later, the Vaticanus manuscript would confirm that Griesbach's choice was correct. Today we have one of the oldest and most valued manuscripts, P^{75}, and it has the shorter reading as well. Many scribes from the fourth century onward harmonized Luke's form of the prayer with Matthew's Gospel.

Luke 11:3-4 New American Standard Bible (NASB / NU)	Luke 11:3-4 New King James Version (NKJV / TR)
³'Give us each day our daily bread. ⁴'And forgive us our sins, For we ourselves also forgive everyone who is indebted to us. And lead us not into temptation.'"	³ Give us day by day our daily bread. ⁴ And forgive us our sins, For we also forgive everyone who is indebted to us. And do not lead us into temptation, **But deliver us from the evil one.**"

Karl Lachmann [1793-1851]

After two and a half centuries, in 1831 a German classical philologist and critic, Karl Lachmann, had the courage to publish an edition of the New Testament text he prepared from his examination of the manuscripts and variants, determining on a case-by-case basis what he believed the original reading was, never beholding to the Textus Receptus. However, he did not include his textual rules and principles in his critical text. He simple stated that these principles could be found in a theological journal. "Karl Lachmann, a classical philologist, produced a fresh text (in 1831) that presented the Greek New Testament of the fourth century."[108]

The *Interpreter's Dictionary of the Bible* sums up Lachmann's six textual criteria as follows:

- Nothing is better attested than that in which all authorities agree.

- The agreement has less weight if part of the authorities are silent or in any way defective.

- The evidence for a reading, when it is that of witnesses of different regions, is greater than that of witnesses of some particular place, differing either from negligence or from set purpose.

- The testimonies are to be regarded as doubtfully balanced when witnesses from widely separated regions stand opposed to others equally wide apart.

- Readings are uncertain which occur habitually in different forms in different regions.

- Readings are of weak authority which are not universally attested in the same region.[109]

It was not Lachmann's intention to restore the text of the New Testament back to the original, as he believed this to be impossible. Rather,

---

[108] (P. Comfort, Encountering the Manuscripts: An Introduction to New Testament Paleography and Textual Criticism 2005, 294)

[109] Biographies of Textual Critics - SkyPoint,
http://www.skypoint.com/members/waltzmn/Bios.html (accessed June 10, 2016).

his intention was to offer a text based solely on documentary evidence, setting aside any text that had been published prior to his, producing a text from the fourth century. Lachmann used no minuscule manuscripts, but instead, he based his text on the Alexandrian text-type, as well as the agreement of the Western authorities, namely, the Old Latin and Greek Western Uncials if the oldest Alexandrian authorities differed. He also used the testimonies of Irenaeus, Origen, Cyprian, Hilary, and Lucifer. As A. T. Robertson put it, Lachman wanted "to get away from the tyranny of the Textus Receptus." Lachmann was correct in that he could not get back to the original, at least for the whole of the NT text, as he simply did not have the textual evidence that we have today, or even what Westcott and Hort had in 1881. Codex Sinaiticus had yet to be discovered, and Codex Vaticanus had yet to be photographed and edited. Moreover, he did not have the papyri that we have today.

Samuel Prideaux Tregelles [1813-1875]

Tregelles was an English Bible scholar, textual critic, and theologian. He was born to Quaker parents at Wodehouse Place, Falmouth on January 30, 1813. He was the son of Samuel Tregelles (1789–1828) and his wife Dorothy (1790–1873). His education began at Falmouth Grammar School. He lost his father at the young age of fifteen, compelling him to take a job at the Neath Abbey iron works. However, he had a gift and a love of language, which led him in his free time to the study of Hebrew, Greek, Aramaic, Latin, and Welsh. He began the study of the New Testament at the age of twenty-five, which would become his life's work.

Tregelles discovered that the Textus Receptus was not based on any ancient witnesses, and he determined that he would publish the Greek text of the New Testament grounded in ancient manuscripts, as well as the citations of the early church fathers, exactly as Karl Lachmann was doing in Germany. In 1845, he spent five months in Rome, hoping to collate Codex Vaticanus in the Vatican Library. Philip W. Comfort writes, "Samuel Tregelles (self-taught in Latin, Hebrew, and Greek) devoted his entire life's work to publishing one Greek text (which came out in six parts, from 1857 to 1872).[110] As is stated in the introduction to this work, Tregelles's goal was 'to exhibit the text of the New Testament in the very words in which it has been transmitted on the evidence of ancient authority.'[111] During this same era, Tischendorf was devoting a lifetime of labor to discovering manuscripts and producing accurate editions of the Greek New Testament."[112]

Friedrich Constantin von Tischendorf [1815-1874]

Tischendorf was a world leading biblical scholar who rejected higher criticism, which led to his noteworthy success in defending the authenticity of the Bible text. He was born in Lengenfeld, Saxony, in northern Europe, the son of a physician, in the year 1815. Tischendorf was educated in Greek at the University of Leipzig. During his university studies, he was troubled by higher criticism of the Bible, as taught by famous German theologians, who sought to prove that the Greek New Testament was not authentic. Tischendorf became convinced, however, that thorough research of the early manuscripts would prove the trustworthiness of the Bible text.

We are indebted to Tischendorf for dedicating his life and abilities to searching through Europe's finest libraries and the monasteries of the Middle East for ancient Bible manuscripts, and especially for rescuing the great Codex Sinaiticus from destruction. However, our highest thanks go to our heavenly Father, who has used hundreds of men since the days of Desiderius Erasmus, who published the first printed Greek New Testament in 1516, so that the Word of God has been accurately preserved for us today. We can be grateful for the women of the twentieth and now the twenty-first century who have given their lives to this great work as well, such as Barbara Aland.

---

[110] Because he was very poor, Tregelles had to ask sponsors to help him with the cost of publishing. The text came out in six volumes over a fifteen-year period—the last being completed just prior to his death. I consider myself fortunate to own a copy of Tregelles's *Greek New Testament* with his signature.

[111] See Prolegomena to Tregelles's *Greek New Testament*.

[112] (P. Comfort, Encountering the Manuscripts: An Introduction to New Testament Paleography and Textual Criticism 2005, 100)

In the second principal recension of Tischendorf (as enumerated in Reuss 1872), the Introduction sets forth the following canons of criticism with examples of their application (see Tregelles 1854, pp. 119-21):

Basic Rule: "The text is only to be sought from ancient evidence, and especially from Greek manuscripts, but without neglecting the testimonies of versions and fathers."

1. "A reading altogether peculiar to one or another ancient document is suspicious; as also is any, even if supported by a class of documents, which seems to evince that it has originated in the revision of a learned man."

2. "Readings, however well supported by evidence, are to be rejected, when it is manifest (or very probable) that they have proceeded from the errors of copyists."

3. "In parallel passages, whether of the New or Old Testament, especially in the Synoptic Gospels, which ancient copyists continually brought into increased accordance, those testimonies are preferable, in which precise accordance of such parallel passages is not found; unless, indeed, there are important reasons to the contrary."

4. "In discrepant readings, that should be preferred which may have given occasion to the rest, or which appears to comprise the elements of the others."

5. "Those readings must be maintained which accord with New Testament Greek, or with the particular style of each individual writer."[113]

Westcott's and Hort's 1881 Master Text

The climax of this restoration era goes to the immediate successors of these men, the two English Bible scholars B. F. Westcott and F. J. A. Hort, upon whose text the United Bible Society is based, which is the foundation for all modern-day translations of the Bible.

---

[113] Bibliography of Textual Criticism "T", http://www.bible-researcher.com/bib-t.html (accessed June 12, 2016).

Westcott and Hort began their work in 1853 and finished it in 1881, working for twenty-eight years independently of each other, yet frequently comparing notes. As the Scottish biblical scholar Alexander Souter expressed it, they "gathered up in themselves all that was most valuable in the work of their predecessors. The maxims which they enunciated on questions of the text are of such importance." (Souter 1913, 118) They took all imaginable factors into consideration in laboring to resolve the difficulties that conflicting texts presented, and when two readings had equal weight, they indicated that in their text. They emphasized, "Knowledge of documents should precede final judgment upon readings" and "all trustworthy restoration of corrupted texts is founded on the study of their history." They followed Griesbach in dividing manuscripts into families, stressing the significance of manuscript genealogy. In addition, they gave due weight to internal evidence, "intrinsic probability" and "transcriptional probability," that is, what the original author most likely wrote and wherein a copyist may most likely have made a mistake.

Westcott and Hort relied heavily on what they called the "neutral" family of texts, which involved the renowned fourth-century vellum Vaticanus and Sinaiticus manuscripts. They considered it quite decisive whenever these two manuscripts agreed, particularly when reinforced by other ancient uncial manuscripts. However, they were not thoughtlessly bound to the Vaticanus manuscript as some scholars have claimed, for by assessing all the elements they frequently concluded that certain minor interpolations had crept into the neutral text that was not found in the group more given to interpolations and paraphrasing, i.e. the Western manuscript family. E. J. Goodspeed has shown that Westcott and Hort departed from Vaticanus seven hundred times in the Gospels alone.

According to Bruce M. Metzger, "the general validity of their critical principles and procedures is widely acknowledged by scholars today." In 1981 Metzger said,

> The international committee that produced the United Bible Societies Greek New Testament, not only adopted the Westcott and Hort edition as its basic text, but followed their methodology in giving attention to both external and internal consideration.

Philip Comfort offered this opinion:

> The text produced by Westcott and Hort is still to this day, even with so many more manuscript discoveries, a very close reproduction of the primitive text of the New Testament. Of course, I think they gave too much weight to Codex Vaticanus alone, and this needs to be tempered. This criticism aside, the

Westcott and Hort text is extremely reliable. (...) In many instances where I would disagree with the wording in the Nestle / UBS text in favor of a particular variant reading, I would later check with the Westcott and Hort text and realize that they had often come to the same decision. (...) Of course, the manuscript discoveries of the past one hundred years have changed things, but it is remarkable how often they have affirmed the decisions of Westcott and Hort.[114]

Critical Rules of Westcott & Hort

The following summary of principles is taken from the compilation in Epp and Fee, *Studies in the Theory and Method of New Testament Textual Criticism* (1993, pages 157-8). References in parentheses are to sections of Hort's *Introduction*, from which the principles have been extracted.

1. Older readings, manuscripts, or groups are to be preferred. ("The shorter the interval between the time of the autograph and the end of the period of transmission in question, the stronger the presumption that earlier date implies greater purity of text.") (2.59; cf. 2.5-6, 31)

2. Readings are approved or rejected by reason of the quality, and not the number, of their supporting witnesses. ("No available presumptions whatever as to text can be obtained from number alone, that is, from number not as yet interpreted by descent.") (2.44)

3. A reading combining two simple, alternative readings is later than the two readings comprising the conflation, and manuscripts rarely or never supporting conflate reading are text antecedent to mixture and are of special value. (2.49-50).

4. The reading is to be preferred that makes the best sense, that is, that best conforms to the grammar and is most congruous with the purport of the rest of the sentence and of the larger context. (2.20)

5. The reading is to be preferred that best conforms to the usual style of the author and to that author's material in other passages. (2.20)

6. The reading is to be preferred that most fitly explains the existence of the others. (2.22-23)

7. The reading is less likely to be original that combines the appearance of an improvement in the sense with the absence of its reality; the scribal

---

[114] Philip Comfort, *Encountering the Manuscripts: An Introduction to New Testament Paleography & Textual Criticism*, (Nashville, 2005), p. 100.

alteration will have an apparent excellence, while the original will have the highest real excellence. (2.27, 29)

8. The reading is less likely to be original that shows a disposition to smooth away difficulties (another way of stating that the harder reading is preferable). (2.28)

9. Readings are to be preferred that are found in a manuscript that habitually contains superior readings as determined by intrinsic and transcriptional probability. Certainty is increased if such a better manuscript is found also to be an older manuscript (2.32-33) and if such a manuscript habitually contains reading that prove themselves antecedent to mixture and independent of external contamination by other, inferior texts (2.150-51). The same principles apply to groups of manuscripts (2.260-61).[115]

Setting Straight the Indefensible Defenders of the Textus Receptus

J. W. Burgon

While Karl Lachmann was the one to overthrow the Textus Receptus, it would be B. F. Westcott and F. J. A. Hort in 1881 who would put the nails in the coffin of the Textus Receptus. The 1881 British Revised Version (RV), also known as the English Revised Version (ERV) of the King James Version, and the 1881 New Testament Greek text of Westcott and Hort did not set well with the King-James-Version-Only[116] advocate John William Burgon (1813–1888), E. H. A. Scrivener (1813–1891), and Edward Miller (1825–1901), the latter authoring *A Guide to the Textual Criticism of the New Testament* (1886). We do not have the space nor the time to offer a full-scale argument against the King James Version Only and the Textus Receptus Only groups. However, we will address what amounts to their

---

[115] Studies in the Theory and Method of New Testament Textual ..., https://www.logos.com/product/46572/studies-in-the-theory-and-method-of-new-test (accessed June 12, 2016).

[116] A connected group of Christians promotes the King James Only movement. It is their position that the King James Version of the Bible is superior to all other English translations, and that all English translations based on the Westcott and Hort text of 1881 (foundation text of UBS5 and NA28) are corrupt due to the influence of the Alexandrian Greek manuscripts.

main arguments. This should help the reader to see how desperate and weak their arguments are.

Bible scholar David Fuller brings us **the first argument** in his book, *Which Bible*, where he writes, "Burgon regarded the good state of preservation of B (Codex Vaticanus) and ALEPH (Codex Sinaiticus) in spite of their exceptional age as proof not of their goodness but of their badness. If they had been good manuscripts, they would have been read to pieces long ago. We suspect that these two manuscripts are indebted for their preservation, solely to their ascertained evil character .... Had B (Vaticanus) and ALEPH (Sinaiticus) been copies of average purity, they must long since have shared the inevitable fate of books which are freely used and highly prized; namely, they would have fallen into decadence and disappeared from sight. Thus, the fact that B and ALEPH are so old is a point against them, not something in their favour. It shows that the Church rejected them and did not read them. Otherwise, they would have worn out and disappeared through much reading."

Thus, Vaticanus and Sinaiticus, leading representatives of the Alexandrian family of manuscripts, are in such great condition because they are full of errors, alterations, additions and deletions, so they would have had little chance of wear and tear, never having been used by true believers. This argument is simply the weakest and most desperate that this author has ever heard. **First**, many of the papyrus Alexandrian manuscripts are in terrible shape, some being 200 years older than codices Vaticanus and Sinaiticus, which would mean that they must have been read very often by true believers. **Second**, a number of old Byzantine and Western manuscripts are in good condition as well, which by this argument would indicate that they are also guilty of never having been read because they were full of errors, alterations, additions and deletions, so they would have had little chance of wear and tear. **Third**, the size of Sinaiticus with the Old Testament, the New Testament, and apocryphal books, among other books would have weighed about 50+ lbs. This book was not read in the same manner that Christians would read their Bibles today. The same would be true of Codex Vaticanus as well. **Fourth**, both were written on extremely expensive and durable calfskin. **Fifth**, the period of copying the Byzantine text type was c. 330 – 1453 C.E. and it progressed into the most corrupt period for the Church (priests to the popes: stealing, sexual sins, torture, and murder); so much so, it ends with the Reformation. Thus, the idea of **true believers** wearing out manuscripts is ludicrous. **Sixth**, the Bible was locked up in Latin. Jerome's Latin Vulgate, produced in the 5th century to make the Bible accessible to all, became a means of keeping God's Word hidden. Almost all Catholic priests were biblically illiterate, so one wonders who were these so-called true believers and how were they reading God's Word to the point of wearing it out. For centuries, manuscripts were preserved, even when the Catholic priests could no longer understand them.

Burgon, Miller, and Scrivener in their **second argument** maintained that the Byzantine text was used by the church for far more centuries, which proved its integrity, as God would never allow the church to use a corrupt text. B. F. Westcott wrote, "A corrupted Bible is a sign of a corrupt church, a Bible mutilated or imperfect, a sign of a church not yet raised to complete perfection of the truth." (*The Bible in the Church*, 1864, 1875) The reader can determine for himself or herself if it is mere coincidence that as the church grew corrupt, the most corrupt manuscript of all grew right along with it for a thousand years.

As was stated earlier, Lucian produced the Syrian text, renamed the Byzantine text. About 290 C.E., some of his associates made various subsequent alterations, which deliberately combined elements from earlier types of text, and this text was adopted about 380 C.E. At Constantinople, it became the predominant form of the New Testament throughout the Greek-speaking world. The text was also edited, with harmonized parallel accounts, grammar corrections, and abrupt transitions modified to produce a smooth text. This was not a faithfully accurate copy. As we had just learned earlier under the corruption period, after Constantine legalized Christianity, giving it equal status with the pagan religions, it was much easier for those possessing manuscripts to have them copied. In fact, Constantine had ordered 50 copies of the whole of the Bible for the church in Constantinople. Over the next four centuries or so, the Byzantine Empire and the Greek-speaking church **were the dominant factors** as to why this area saw their text becoming the standard. It had nothing to do with it being the better text, i.e., the text that more accurately reflected the original. From the eighth century forward, the corrupt Byzantine text was the standard text and had displaced all others; it makes up about 95 percent of all manuscripts that we have of the Christian Greek Scriptures.

Burgon, Miller, and Scrivener in their **third argument** continued with the belief that it would be foolish to set aside thousands of manuscript witnesses (the Byzantine text-type) for a few *supposedly* early manuscript witnesses (the Alexandrian text-type). But in truth, the majority of anything does not automatically mean that it is the best or even correct. Today we can easily produce thousands of copies of a faulty manuscript with a machine, and every copy displays the same errors. If we were to hand-copy the same manuscript a thousand times, obvious errors probably would be corrected in many copies, but new errors would be introduced, many of them probably the result of a well-intended "correction." A textual criticism principle that has been derived from this observation is that manuscripts should be weighed (i.e. for value), not counted.

In their **fourth argument,** Burgon, Miller, and Scrivener maintained that the Byzantine text-type was actually older and superior to the Alexandrian text-type. To refute this, we can go back to our patristic quotations, which reveal the Alexandrian text-type as earlier than the Byzantine text-type. Greenlee writes, "The fallacy in this argument was that the antiquity of a 'Syrian' (i.e., Byzantine) reading could be shown only when the Byzantine text was supported by one of the pre-Byzantine texts, which proved nothing in favor of the Byzantine, since WH maintained that Syrian readings were largely derived from the pre-Syrian texts. That the traditional text was intrinsically superior was more nearly a matter of subjective opinion; but extensive comparison of text-types has left most scholars convinced that the late text [Byzantine] is in general inferior, not superior."[117]

Metzger (whom I cite at length) writes,

> The Alexandrian text, which Westcott and Hort called the Neutral text (a question-begging title), is usually considered to be the best text and the most faithful in preserving the original. Characteristics of the Alexandrian text are brevity and austerity. That is, it is generally shorter than the text of other forms, and it does not exhibit the degree of grammatical and stylistic polishing that is characteristic of the Byzantine type of text. Until recently the two chief witnesses to the Alexandrian text were codex Vaticanus (B) and codex Sinaiticus (א), parchment manuscripts dating from about the middle of the fourth century. With the acquisition, however, of the Bodmer Papyri, particularly P^{66} and P^{75}, both copied about the end of the second or the beginning of the third century, evidence is now available that the Alexandrian type of text goes back to an archetype that must be dated early in the second century. The Sahidic and Bohairic versions frequently contain typically Alexandrian readings .... It was the corrupt Byzantine form of text that provided the basis for almost all translations of the New Testament into modern languages down to the nineteenth century. During the eighteenth century scholars assembled a great amount of information from many Greek manuscripts, as well as from versional and patristic witnesses. But, except for three or four editors who timidly corrected some of the more blatant errors of the Textus Receptus, this debased form of the

---

[117] (Greenlee, Introduction to New Testament Textual Criticism 1995, 76-7)

New Testament text was reprinted in edition after edition. It was only in the first part of the nineteenth century (1831) that a German classical scholar, Karl Lachmann, ventured to apply to the New Testament the criteria that he had used in editing texts of the classics. Subsequently other critical editions appeared, including those prepared by Constantin von Tischendorf, whose eighth edition (1869–72) remains a monumental thesaurus of variant readings, and the influential edition prepared by two Cambridge scholars, B. F. Westcott and F. J. A. Hort (1881). It is the latter edition that was taken as the basis for the present United Bible Societies' edition. During the twentieth century, with the discovery of several New Testament manuscripts much older than any that had hitherto been available, it has become possible to produce editions of the New Testament that approximate ever more closely to what is regarded as the wording of the original documents.[118]

History of the Nestle-Aland Edition

It seems best to allow the German Bible Society and the Institute for New Testament Textual Research to tell their own history:

In 1898, Eberhard Nestle published the first edition of his Novum Testamentum Graece. Based on a simple yet ingenious idea it disseminated the insights of the textual criticism of that time through a hand edition designed for university and school studies and for church purposes. Nestle took the three leading scholarly editions of the Greek New Testament at that time by Tischendorf, Westcott/Hort and Weymouth as a basis. (After 1901 he replaced the latter with Bernhard Weiß's 1894/1900 edition.) Where their textual decisions differed from each other Nestle chose for his own text the variant which was preferred by two of the editions included, while the variant of the third was put into the apparatus.

The text-critical apparatus remained rudimentary in all the editions published by Eberhard Nestle. It was Eberhard Nestle's son Erwin who provided the 13th edition of 1927 with a consistent critical apparatus

---

[118] Bruce Manning Metzger, United Bible Societies, *A Textual Commentary on the Greek New Testament, Second Edition a Companion Volume to the United Bible Societies' Greek New Testament (4th Rev. Ed.)* (London; New York: United Bible Societies, 1994), xx, xxv.

 showing evidence from manuscripts, early translations and patristic citations. However, these notes did not derive from the primary sources, but only from editions.

This changed in the nineteen-fifties, when Kurt Aland started working for the edition by checking the apparatus entries against Greek manuscripts and editions of the Church Fathers. This phase came to a close in 1963 when the 25th edition of the Novum Testamentum Graece appeared; later printings of this edition already carried the brand name "Nestle-Aland" on their covers.

The 26th edition, which appeared in 1979, featured a fundamentally new approach. Until then the guiding principle had been to adopt the text supported by a majority of the critical editions referred to. Now the text was established on the basis of source material that had been assembled and evaluated in the intervening period. It included early papyri and other manuscript discoveries, so that the 26th edition represented the situation of textual criticism in the 20th century. Its text was identical with that of the 3rd edition of the UBS Greek New Testament (GNT) published in 1975, as a consequence of the parallel work done on both editions. Already in 1955 Kurt Aland was invited to participate in an editorial committee with Matthew Black, Bruce M. Metzger, Alan Wikgren, and at first Arthur Vööbus, later Carlo Martini (and, from 1982, Barbara Aland and Johannes Karavidopoulos) to produce a reliable hand edition of the Greek New Testament.

The first edition of the GNT appeared in 1966. Its text was established along the lines of Westcott and Hort and differed considerably from Nestle's 25th edition. This holds true for the second edition of the GNT as well. When the third edition was prepared Kurt Aland was able to contribute the textual proposals coming from his preliminary work on the 26th edition of the Nestle-Aland. Hence the process of establishing the text for both editions continued to converge, so that eventually they could share an identical text. However, their external appearance and the design of their apparatus remains different, because they serve different purposes. The GNT is primarily intended for translators, providing a reliable Greek initial text and a text-critical apparatus showing variants that are relevant for translation. In the case of the passages selected for this purpose the evidence is displayed as completely as possible. The Novum Testamentum Graece is produced primarily for research, academic education and pastoral practice. It seeks to provide an apparatus that enables the reader to make a critical assessment of the reconstruction of the Greek initial text.

The text of the 26th edition of the Nestle-Aland was adopted for the 27th edition also, while the apparatus underwent an extensive revision. The text remained the same, because the 27th edition was not "deemed an appropriate occasion for introducing textual changes". Since then the situation has changed, because the Editio Critica Maior (ECM) of the Catholic Letters is now available. Its text was established on the basis of all the relevant material from manuscripts and other sources. The ECM text was adopted for the present edition following approval by the editorial committee of the Nestle-Aland and the GNT.[119]

This makes more certain for us the Apostle Peter's words: "But the word of the Lord endures forever." (1 Peter 1:25, NASB) We can have the same confidence that the One who inspired the Holy Scriptures, giving us His inerrant Word, has also used his servants to preserve them throughout the last two thousand years, "who desires all men to be saved and to come to the knowledge of the truth." (1 Tim. 2:4, NASB) The beloved Bruce Manning Metzger was right; the text of the New Testament was transmitted; then, it entered a 1,400-year period of corruption, and has been enjoying a 500-year period of restoration.

Chapter 10 is not meant to be cruel. The King James version served us well for 400 years. However, so did the horse and plow. But when we get the modern-day farm equipment that can take care of thousands of acres, we do not stay with the horse and plow. The same holds true, many hundreds have given their lives to bring us translations that are mirror-like reflections of the originals in our language.

---

[119] Nestle Aland Novum Testamentum Graece: History, http://www.nestle-aland.com/en/history/ (accessed June 12, 2016).

CHAPTER 10 The Reign of the King James Version Is Over

Exactly why are we making other translations beyond the King James Version of 1611? The King James Version has been the primary translation of the Christian community for 400 years (1611-2011). There is no doubt that this Bible alone has affected the lives of hundreds of millions and has influenced the principles of Bible translation for the past four centuries.

Before we delve into what makes for a good translation, let us pause to consider the translation policy of the KJV translation committee. We can hardly talk about the KJV without looking at the translator William Tyndale (1494-1536), the man who published the first printed New Testament from the original language of Greek. In the face of much persecution, William Tyndale of England followed with his English translation of Erasmus' Greek New Testament text, completing this while in exile on the continent of Europe in 1525.

Tyndale respected and treasured the Bible. However, in his days, the religious leaders insisted on keeping it in Latin, a language that had been dead for centuries. Therefore, with the purpose of making it available to his fellow citizens, Tyndale was determined to translate the Bible into English. While the idea of Bible translation being against the law may be unfamiliar to the modern mind, this was not the case in Tyndale's day. He was educated at Oxford University and became an esteemed instructor at The Cambridge University. Because of his desire to bring the common man the Bible in English, he had to flee from his academic career, escaping the Continent. His life became one of a fugitive, but he managed to complete the New Testament and some of the Old Testament, before he was finally arrested, imprisoned for heresy, and strangled at the stake, with his body being burned afterward.

Tyndale's work sparked a widespread translation project that produced a new revision every couple of years, or so it seemed. The Coverdale Bible of 1536, the Matthew's Bible of 1537, the Great Bible of 1539, the Taverner's Bible of 1539, the Geneva Bible of 1560 (went through 140 editions), the Edmund Becke's Bible of 1549, the Bishop's Bible of 1568, and the Rheims-Douay Bible of 1610. The King James Version is a revision of all these translations, as they too were of their predecessor, the Tyndale translation. The KJV translation committee was ordered to use the Bishop's Bible as their foundation text and was not to alter it unless Tyndale, Coverdale, Matthew, Cranmer or the Great Bible, and the Geneva agreed, and then they were to assume that reading. Thus, the King James Version is unquestionably 90 percent William Tyndale's translation.

There is no other translation, which possesses more literary beauty than the King James Version. However, there are several reasons as to why there was a need to revise the King James Version. The **first reason** is the **King James Version's** textual basis, which is from the period of 1611. The Greek text behind the KJV New Testament is what is known as the Textus Receptus, a corrupt Greek text produced by a scholar in the 16th-century, Desiderius Erasmus. Concerning this text, Dr. Bruce Metzger wrote that it was "a handful of late and haphazardly collected minuscule manuscripts and in a dozen passages its reading is supported by no Greek witnesses." (Metzger 2003, 106) While most of the corruptions are considered insignificant, others are significant, such as 1 Timothy 3:16; 1 John 5:7; John 7:53-8:11; and Mark 16:9-20. However, we cannot lay the blame at the feet of the translation committee of the KJV, for they did not have the textual evidence that we possess today.

The **second reason** is that the **KJV** comes from the 17th-century and contains many archaic words that either obscure the meaning or mislead its reader: "howbeit." "thee," "thy," "thou," "thine," and "shambles." An example of misleading can be found in the word "let," which meant to "stop," "hinder" or "restrain" in 1611, but today means "to allow" or "to permit." Therefore, when the KJV says that Paul 'let the great apostasy come into the church,' it is completely misleading to the modern mind. In 1611 "let" meant that he 'restrained or prevented the apostasy.' (2 Thess. 2:7) The KJV at Mark 6:20 inform us "Herod feared John, knowing that he was a just man and an holy, and observed him." Actually, the Greek behind "observed him" means that Herod "kept him safe."

The **third reason** is that the **KJV** contains translation errors. However, like the first reason, it is not the fault of the translators, as Hebrew and Greek were just resurfacing as subjects of serious study after the Dark Ages. The discovery of papyrus writings in Egypt, in the late 19th and early 20th centuries, has helped us better to understand the common (Koine) Greek of the first century C.E. These discoveries have shown that everyday words were not understood as well as had been thought. The KJV at Matthew 5:22 informs the reader "whosoever is angry with his brother without a cause shall be in danger of the judgment: and whosoever shall say to his brother, Raca, shall be in danger of the council ..." The ESV renders it, "whoever insults his brother will be liable (a term of abuse) to the council ..." Scholar Walter C. Kaiser has said, "the actual insult mentioned by Jesus is the word 'Raca' as it stands in the KJV. The precise meaning of 'Raca' is disputed; it is probably an Aramaic word meaning something like 'imbecile' but was plainly regarded as a deadly insult."

The **fourth reason** is that the **KJV** has over a thousand words in it that do not mean today what they meant in 1611. Words change over time, some even meaning the opposite. For example, the word "let," as used in the King James Version, meant 'to stop,' 'to prevent,' or 'to restrain' in 1611. Today "let" means 'to allow,' 'to permit,' or 'consent to. Thus, in 1611, when the KJV was published, 2 Thessalonians said that Paul "let" the great apostasy come into the church, which meant that Paul actually "stopped" or "restrained" the great apostasy from coming into the church. Now, those who do not know that in 1611 "let" meant, "prevent," "stop," and "restrain" in 1611, it was correctly translated. However, today, the English reader would be getting the opposite meaning from that 2 Thessalonians 2:7.

2 Thessalonians 2:7 Updated American Standard Version (UASV)	2 Thessalonians 2:7 King James Version (KJV)
[7] For the mystery[120] of lawlessness is already at work; but only until	[7] For the mystery of iniquity doth already work: only he who now

---

[120] **Mystery; Secret**: (Gr. *mystērion*) A sacred divine mystery or secret doctrine that lies with God alone, which is withheld from both the angelic body and humans, until the time he determines that it is to be revealed, and to those to whom he chooses to make it known.–

the one who is right now acting as a restraint is out of the way.	letteth will let, until he be taken out of the way.

The translators that have come after the King James Version can draw much direction in what makes a worthy translation by considering the principles of translation that were followed in the production of the world's most influential Bible. The translators endeavored to discover the corresponding English word for the actual original language word of Hebrew and Greek.

According to Alister McGrath, the translators felt obligated to . . .

- Ensure that every word in the original was rendered by an English equivalent;
- Make it clear when they added any words to make the sense clearer, or to lead to better English . . .
- Follow the basic word order of the original wherever possible.[121]

There is any number of ways that each one of us may have been drawn into the field of Bible translation differences, the translation process, and textual criticism. It might be that some have been using the King James Version their entire life and with all of these new translations reading differently, especially in the New Testament, they began investigating why. Maybe it is the opposite, and we are using a more recent English translation such as the NASB, ESV, HCSB, LEB or the UASV. Then, maybe we have had a number of persons, who are commonly called the King James Version Only tell us that the KJV is based on the best and oldest Greek manuscripts, saying our translation is corrupt. Thus, in either of the above scenarios, we began by comparing the King James Version with some of the New Translations. We began to discover many differences between the new translations and the King James Version, which made us wonder, which is correct? We wonder, "Is the Bible that I have been using even accurate?" or "How can I know which Bible translation is most accurate?" Below are but a few examples **out of hundreds** of what would be discovered upon such an investigation. In our examples, we have chosen to compare the King James Version (KJV, 1611) against the Updated American Standard Version (UASV, 2016). Keep in mind that the 1901 ASV, the 1952 RSV, the

---

Mark 4:11; Rom. 11:25; 16:25; 1 Cor. 2:1; 4:1; 13:2; 14:2; 15:51; Eph. 1:9; 6:19; Col. 1:26; 2:2; 2 Thess. 2:7; 1 Tim. 3:9; Rev. 17:5.

[121] McGrath, Alister. *In the Beginning: The Story of the King James Bible and How It Changed a Nation, a Language, and a Culture.* New York: Anchor, 2002, p. 250.

1995 NASB, and the 2001 ESV are going to read similar to the UASV because they too are literal translations based on the latest and best evidence. (some not as literal as the UASV, e.g., the ESV, RSV) The **Textus Receptus** (i.e., received text) is the name given to the printed Greek text of the New Testament, which served as the basis for the original German Luther Bible (1522), the translation of the New Testament into English by William Tyndale (1526), the King James Version (1611), and most other New Testament translations of the Reformation era. The critical Greek texts of the New Testament, which has served as the basis for modern-day translations, including the ESV, are the Westcott and Hort Text of 1881, the United Bible Society (UBS5, 2014), and the Nestle-Aland (NA28, 2012).[122] Material within brackets [ ] means the reading was not in the original text.

Matthew 5:44

KJV: But I say unto you, Love your enemies, bless them that curse you, do good to them that hate you, and pray for them which despitefully use you, and persecute you;

UASV: But I say to you, Love your enemies and pray for those who persecute you,

[do good to them that hate you, and pray for them which despitefully use you, and persecute you;] The shorter reading in the ESV is found in the more trusted manuscripts from the fourth century while the longer reading of the KJV is found in manuscripts of the fifth century and beyond. The shorter reading is found in the citation of earlier church fathers while later church fathers cited the longer reading. It seems a copyist borrowed the above words from Luke 6:27-28, adding them to Matthew.

Matthew 6:13

KJV: And lead us not into temptation, but deliver us from evil: For thine is the kingdom, and the power, and the glory, forever. Amen.

UASV: And lead us not into temptation, but deliver us from evil.

[For thine is the kingdom, and the power, and the glory, forever. Amen.] The manuscript evidence is against the longer reading being original. It likely came from the *Didache* (aka, The Teaching of the Twelve Apostles) which is a brief early Christian source on traditions of the church, dated by most scholars to the early second century.

---

[122] The primary difference between the UBS5 and the NA28 is that translators primarily use the latter, while textual scholars primarily use the former.

Matthew 17:21

KJV: Howbeit this kind goeth not out but by prayer and fasting.

UASV: The verse was omitted because of the substantial manuscript evidence led to the conclusion that this verse was not in the original text.

Bruce M. Metzger observes, "There is no satisfactory reason why the passage, if originally present in Matthew, should have been omitted in a wide variety of witnesses, and ... copyists frequently inserted material derived from another Gospel ..."[4]

Matthew 18:11

KJV: For the Son of man is come to save that which was lost.

UASV: The verse was omitted because it was absent from several important and diverse manuscripts, evidencing that this verse was not in the original text.

On this verse, Metzger writes, "There can be little doubt that the words [from the longer reading] are spurious here, being absent from the earliest witnesses representing several textual types (Alexandrian, Egyptian, Antiochian), and manifestly borrowed by copyists from Lk 19:10. The reason for the interpolation was apparently to provide a connection between ver. 10 and verses 12–14."[5]

What Was a Pim?

1 Samuel 13:21 King James Version (KJV)

²¹ Yet they had a file [Heb., *pim*] for the mattocks, and for the coulters, and for the forks, and for the axes, and to sharpen the goads.

1 Samuel 13:21 Updated American Standard Version (UASV)

²¹ The charge was a pim[6] for the plowshares and for the mattocks, for the three-pronged fork, for the axes, and for fixing the oxgoad.

1 Samuel 13:21 English Standard Version (ESV)

²¹ and the charge was two-thirds of a shekel for the plowshares and for the mattocks, and a third of a shekel for sharpening the axes and for setting the goads.

1 Samuel 13:21 New American Standard Bible (NASB)

²¹ The charge was two-thirds of a shekel for the plowshares, the mattocks, the forks, and the axes, and to fix the hoes.

What was a pim? It would not be uncovered until 1907 when archaeology discovered the first pim weight stone at the ancient city of Gezer. The translation, like the above King James Version, struggled in their translation of the word "pim." Today, translators know that the pim was a weight measure of about 7.82 grams, or as the English Standard Version has it, "two-thirds of a shekel," a common Hebrew unit of weight that the Philistines charged for sharpening the Israelites plowshares and mattocks.

Weight inscribed with the word pym Z.

Radovan/www.BibleLandPictures.com[7]

What is the Mystery of Godliness?

1 Timothy 3:16 Updated American Standard Version (UASV)	1 Timothy 3:16 King James Version (KJV)
[16] And confessedly, great is the mystery of godliness: **He was manifested in the flesh,** vindicated in the Spirit, seen by angels, proclaimed among the nations, believed on in the world, taken up in glory.	[16] And without controversy great is the mystery of godliness: **God was manifest in the flesh,** justified in the Spirit, seen of angels, preached unto the Gentiles, believed on in the world, received up into glory.

The word translated God was originally abbreviated ΘC (the nomen sacrum for θεός), which had originally looked like the Greek word OC (i.e., ὅς), the latter meaning "who." Metzger makes the following observation, "The reading θεός arose either (a) accidentally, through the misreading of OC as ΘC, or (b) deliberately, either to supply a substantive for the following six verbs or, with less probability, to provide greater dogmatic precision." (p. 574) Point (a) that it was an accidental misreading of OC as ΘC and that it was unlikely to be intentional, for doctrinal purposes, seems a bit dismissive. Nevertheless, this has long been the position of many scholars.

In fact, Johann Jakob Wettstein (1693-1754) noticed that ΘC, had originally looked like OC, but felt that a horizontal stroke had faintly shown through the other side of the uncial manuscript page, contributing to a later hand adding a horizontal line to OC, giving us the contraction ΘC ("God"). However, this author believes that Philip W. Comfort makes a valid point, when he writes, "It is difficult to imagine how several fourth-and-fifth-century scribes, who had seen thousands of nomina sacra, would have made this mistake. It is more likely that the changes were motivated by a desire to make the text say that it was "God" who was manifested in the flesh." (P. W. Comfort 2008, 663) If we believe that doctrinal considerations were not behind the scribal changes, all we have to do is investigate what took place when it was understood that the actual reading was "**He who** was manifested in the flesh," as opposed to "**God** was manifested in the flesh." The battle in the nineteenth century was as though the loss of the reading in the Textus Receptus (θεός KJV) would undermine the doctrine of the Trinity. Doctrinal motivations have always played a role in the copying of the Bible, but the truth is these are actually few in number. Considering the number of manuscripts that were copied, if this were a major problem, we should see more.

Scribal Interpolations

1 John 5:7-8 (WHNU)	1 John 5:7-8 (TR)
⁷ οτι τρεις εισιν οι μαρτυρουντες ⁸ το πνευμα και το υδωρ και το αιμα και οι τρεις εις το εν εισιν	⁷ οτι τρεις εισιν οι μαρτυρουντες **εν τω ουρανω ο πατηρ ο λογος και το αγιον** πνευμα και ουτοι οι τρεις εν εισιν

	⁸ καὶ τρεις εισιν οι μαρτυρουντες εν τη γη το πνευμα και το υδωρ και το αιμα και οι τρεις εις το εν εισιν
1 John 5:7-8 (UASV) ⁷ For there are three that testify:¹²³ ⁸ the Spirit and the water and the blood; and the three are in agreement.	**1 John 5:7-8 (KJV)** ⁷ For there are three that bear record **in heaven, the Father, the Word, and the Holy Ghost: and these three are one.** ⁸ And there are three that bear witness **in earth**, the Spirit, and the water, and the blood: and these three agree in one.

In verse 7 of 1 John 5, after μαρτυροῦντες (testify), the Textus Receptus adds, ἐν τῷ οὐρανῷ, ὁ Πατήρ, ὁ Λόγος, καὶ τὸ Ἅγιον Πνεῦμα· καὶ οὗτοι οἱ τρεῖς ἕν εἰσι (in heaven, the Father, the Word, and the Holy Ghost: and these three are one). In verse 8, the Textus Receptus has καὶ τρεῖς εἰσιν οἱ μαρτυροῦντες ἐν τῇ γῇ (And there are three that bear witness in earth). There is no doubt that these words are an interpolation into the text, which textual scholarship has long known.

These additional words are missing from every Greek manuscript except eight, the earliest being from the tenth century. Metzger offers that these eight

After μαρτυροῦντες, the Textus Receptus adds the following: ἐν τῷ οὐρανῷ, ὁ Πατήρ, ὁ Λόγος, καὶ τὸ Ἅγιον Πνεῦμα· καὶ οὗτοι οἱ τρεῖς ἕν εἰσι. (8) καὶ τρεῖς εἰσιν οἱ μαρτυροῦντες ἐν τῇ γῇ. That these words are spurious and have no right to stand in the New Testament is certain in the light of the following considerations. "Contain the passage in what appears to be a translation from a late recension of the Latin Vulgate. Four of the eight manuscripts contain the passage as a variant reading written in the margin as a later addition to the manuscript." (TCGNT, 649)

In addition, the added words were not quoted by any of the Greek Fathers. Certainly, had they been aware of these words, there is little doubt that they would have referenced them repeatedly in the fourth century

---

[123] A few late MSS add ... in heaven, the Father, the Word, and the Holy Spirit, and these three are one. (8) And there are three that testify on earth, the Spirit

Trinitarian debates. Metzger tells us that "Its first appearance in Greek is in a Greek version of the (Latin) Acts of the Lateran Council in 1215." (TCGNT, 649)

The interpolation is also missing from all the manuscripts of the ancient versions, with the exception of the Latin (Syriac, Coptic, Armenian, Ethiopic, Arabic, and Slavonic). However, it is not found in the Old Latin in its earliest form (Tertullian Cyprian Augustine). Moreover, it is not present in "the Vulgate (*b*) as issued by Jerome (codex Fuldensis [copied a.d.541–46] and codex Amiatinus [copied before a.d. 716]) or (*c*) as revised by Alcuin (first hand of codex Vallicellianus [ninth century])." (TCGNT, 649)

This interpolation had its beginning in Latin, in the treatise Liber Apologetics, which was written by the Spanish heretic Priscillian (d. c. 385), bishop of Ávila, or his follower, Bishop Instantius. Metzger writes, "Apparently the gloss arose when the original passage was understood to symbolize the Trinity (through the mention of three witnesses: the Spirit, the water, and the blood), an interpretation that may have been written first as a marginal note that afterward found its way into the text. In the fifth century the gloss was quoted by Latin Fathers in North Africa and Italy as part of the text of the Epistle, and from the sixth century onwards it is found more and more frequently in manuscripts of the Old Latin and of the Vulgate." (TCGNT, 649)

Think about it, if these interpolations were original, there would be no reason to remove them, and they would be found in our earliest and best manuscripts, as well as hundreds of years of copying. Moreover, there would be no reason for their being missing from the versions either. Lastly, the interpolation also interrupts the sense.

Both a Science and an Art

We said at the outset that New Testament textual criticism is both a science and an art. Throughout almost all of this publication, we have used the science aspect, in that we have spoken of and applied many of the rules and principles. However, we will offer one verse here where the art aspect comes into play; we must not be rigid in our application of the rules and principles, meaning that we must be balanced.

Mark 1:41 (TR WHNU)	Mark 1:41 (LEB NEB REB)
σπλαγχνισθεις εκτεινας την χειρα αυτου ηψατο	οργισθεις εκτεινας την χειρα αυτου ηψατο

(א A B C L W f¹,¹³ 33 565 700 syr cop Diatessaron)	(D a, d, ff²)
Mark 1:41 (NASB) ⁴¹ Moved with compassion [*splanchnon*], Jesus stretched out His hand and touched him	Mark 1:41 (LEB) ⁴¹ And becoming angry [*orgistheis*], he stretched out his hand *and* touched *him*

The reason that this text is considered difficult is because of one having to go against the grain of the textual principles: *Which reading is it that the other reading(s) most likely came from?* Well, it is certainly easy to see how "moved with anger" would have been changed to "move with pity." In that case, the scribe would have been softening the reading. It is very difficult to understand why a scribe would be tempted to go from "move with pity" to "moved with anger." On the other hand, the textual evidence for "moved with pity" is very weighty, while the textual evidence "moved with anger" has no real weight at all. Most persons who define textual criticism say, 'it is an art and a science.' What they mean is that it is a science in that there are rules and principles, like the ones above, and it is an art, because one needs to be balanced in the application of those rules and principles. The textual rule of which reading is it that the others came from is not to be rigidly applied; there are times that it does not apply, this being one of them.

First, the Western text **D**, which gives us the reading of "moved with anger," is notorious for making "significant" changes to the text. Comfort and Metzger, as well as others, offer a very real reason as to why the scribe may have chosen to do so. "He may have decided to make Jesus angry with the leper for wanting a miracle–in keeping with the tone of voice Jesus used in 1:43 when he sternly warned the leper." (P. W. Comfort 2008, 98) However, as Comfort goes on to point out, this would have been a misunderstanding on the part of the scribe, because Jesus was not warning him about seeking a miracle, it was rather "a warning about keeping the miracle a secret." Another motive for the scribe to alter the text to the harder reading is because he felt the man was slow to believe that Jesus was serious about healing him (v. 40) In addition, why would the scribes soften the text here from "move with anger" to "moved with pity," but not do the same at Mark 3:12 and 10:14? Let us revisit Erasmus and build on his account, moving on to the critical text.

We can grow in knowledge and understanding of how the Greek New Testament came down to us. If we cannot defend the Bible how can we defend the faith? It is not about winning arguments; it is about winning misguided souls that have been misinformed (1 Pet 3:15) and saving those who have begun to doubt. (Jude 1:22-23)

Why We Can Have Confidence?

The art and science of textual criticism and related areas like paleography go back hundreds of years. Over the last 140-years, textual research has become more certain and exact every year. And each new literal Bible translation that builds upon this foundation in an honest impartial manner, becomes purer and more accurate. Thus, the last 400 years, especially the last 140-years can give us complete confidence that the literal Bible translations are a mirror-like reflection of the originals, the unaltered Word of God.

Chapter 11 will go into an idea that most have never pondered. Do we need to find the original manuscripts to have the originals?

CHAPTER 11 Why Do We Not Need the Original Bible Manuscripts?

Between 3,500 years ago and 2,460 years ago some 32+ authors penned 39 books in the Middle East, compiling a history of the world from its creation, to the flood of Noah, the confusing of the languages at Babylon, Abraham entering Canaan, to the formation of the Israelite nation, to the rise and fall of the Egyptian, Assyrian, Babylonian, Medo-Persian Empires. These 39 books became the most important collection of literature that the world has ever known. They would soon be joined by another 27 books, the second most important collection that was written some 2,000 years ago, covering the birth of the Roman Empire and the birth of the Son of God, as well as the birth and foundation of Christianity.

There was something different about this library of sixty-six books that had been penned over a 1600-year period. The authors came from every walk of life from lowly fisherman and shepherds to a military general, a physician, a tax collector, kings, and the like. These 40+ men were moved along by the Holy Spirit so that what they produced was not theirs alone but belong to one author, the Creator of all thing, God himself. This means that these sixty-six books possessed perfect content (fully inerrant/infallible) with no errors, mistakes, contradictions. We still have translations of these writings today that can be read by almost everyone on earth. However, a question arises because the copyists who were making copies for thousands of years were not moved along by the Holy Spirit. We do not have the original manuscripts. We know that the thousands upon thousands of original language manuscripts (Hebrew OT/Greek NT) and the versions all read differently, as there are hundreds of thousands of scribal errors.[124] How can we be certain that what we have in our Bible translations is really an accurate translation of what the authors originally wrote?

How Our Bible Manuscripts Survived the Elements

One may wonder why more Old and New Testament manuscripts have not survived. Really, the better question would be how come so many of our Bible manuscripts survived in comparison to secular ancient manuscripts? The primary materials used to receive writing in ancient times were perishable papyrus and parchment. It must be remembered that the Christians suffered intense persecution during intervals in the first 300 years from Pentecost 33 C.E. With this persecution from the Roman Empire came

---

[124] https://christianpublishinghouse.co/2017/03/31/what-are-textual-variants-and-how-many-are-there/

many orders to destroy Christian texts. In addition, these texts were not stored in such a way as to secure their preservation; they were actively used by the Christians in the congregation and were subject to wear and tear. Furthermore, moisture is the enemy of papyrus, and it causes them to disintegrate over time. This is why, as we will discover, the papyrus manuscripts that have survived have come from the dry sands of Egypt. Moreover, it seems not to have entered the minds of the early Christians to preserve their documents, because their solution to the loss of manuscripts was just to make more copies. Fortunately, the process of making copies transitioned to the more durable animal skins, which would last much longer. Those that have survived, especially from the fourth century C.E. and earlier, are the path to restoring the original Greek New Testament.[125]

Both papyrus and parchment jeopardized the survival of the Bible because they were perishable materials. Papyrus, the weakest of the two, can tear and discolor. Because of moist climates, a sheet of papyrus can decay to the point where it is nothing more than a handful of dust. We must remember papyrus is a plant and when the scroll has been stored, it can grow mold and it can rot from dampness. It can even be eaten by starving rodents or also insects, especially white ants (i.e., termites) when it has been buried. When some of the manuscripts were first discovered early on, they were exposed to excessive light and humidity, which hastened their deterioration.

While parchment is far more durable than papyrus, it will also perish in time if mishandled or exposed to the elements (temperature, humidity, and light) over time.[126] Parchment is made from animal skin, so it too is also a victim of insects. Hence, when it comes to ancient records, *Everyday Writing in the Graeco-Roman East* states, "survival is the exception rather than the rule." (R. S. Bagnall 2009, 140) Think about it for a moment; the Bible and its special revelation could have died from decay in the elements.

The Mosaic Law commanded every future king, "And when he sits on the throne of his kingdom, he shall write for himself in a book a copy of this law, approved by the Levitical priests." (Deuteronomy 17:18) Moreover, the professional copyist of the Hebrew Old Testament made so many manuscripts, by the time of Jesus and the apostles, throughout all of Israel and even into distant Macedonia, there were many copies of the

---

[125] Cf. J. H. Greenlee, *Introduction to New Testament Textual Criticism* (Peabody: Hendrickson, 1995), 11.

[126] For example, the official signed copy of the U.S. Declaration of Independence was written on parchment. Now, less than 250 years later, it has faded to the point of being barely legible.

Scriptures in the synagogues (Luke 4:16, 17; Acts 17:11) How did our Hebrew Old Testament and Greek New Testament survive the elements to the point where there are far more of them than any other ancient document. For example, there are 5,830+ New Testament manuscripts in the original Greek alone.

New Testament scholar Philip W. Comfort writes, "Jews were known to put scrolls containing Scripture in pitchers or jars in order to preserve them. The Dead Sea scrolls found in jars in the Qumran caves are a celebrated example of this. The Beatty Papyri were very likely a part of a Christian library, which was hidden in jars to be preserved from confiscation during the Diocletian persecution."[127] Christianity were initially made up Jewish Christians only for the first seven years (29-36 C.E.), with Cornelius being the first Gentile baptized in 36 C.E. Much of early Christianity (33-350 C.E.) was made up of Jewish Christians, who evidently carried over the tradition of putting "scrolls containing Scripture in pitchers or jars in order to preserve them." It is for this reason that some of our earliest Bible manuscripts have been discovered in unusually dry regions, in clay jars and even dark closets and caves.

Manuscripts Saved from Egyptian Garbage Heaps

Beginning in 1778 and continuing to the end of the 19th century, many papyrus texts were accidentally discovered in Egypt that dated from 300 B.C.E. to 500 C.E., almost 500 thousand documents in all. About 130 years ago, there began a systematic search. At that time, a continuous flow of ancient texts was being found by the native fellahin, and the Egypt Exploration Society, a British non-profit organization, founded in 1882, realized that they needed to send out an expedition team before it was too late. They sent two Oxford scholars, Bernard P. Grenfell and Arthur S. Hunt, who received permission to search the area south of the farming region in the Faiyūm district. Grenfell chose a site called Behnesa because of its ancient Greek name, Oxyrhynchus. A search of the graveyards and the ruined houses produced nothing. The only place left to search was the town's garbage dumps, which were some 30 feet [9 m] high. It seems to Grenfell and Hunt that all was lost but they decided to try.

In January of 1897, a trial trench (excavation or depression in the ground) was dug, and it only took a few hours before ancient papyrus

---

[127] Philip Wesley Comfort and David P. Barrett, *The Text of the Earliest New Testament Greek Manuscripts* (Wheaton, IL: Tyndale House, 2001), 158.

materials were found. These included letters, contracts, and official documents. The sand had blown over them, covering them, and for nearly 2,000 years, the dry climate had served as a protection for them.

It took only a mere three months to pull out and recover almost two tons of papyri from Oxyrhynchus. They shipped twenty-five large cases back to England. Over the next ten years, these two courageous scholars returned each and every winter, to grow their collection. They discovered ancient classical writing, along with royal ordinances and contracts mixed in with business accounts private letters, shipping lists, as well as fragments of many New Testament manuscripts.

Of what benefit were all these documents? Foremost, the bulk of these documents were written by ordinary people in Koine (common) Greek of the day. Many of the words that would be used in the marketplace, not by the elites appeared in the Greek New Testament Scriptures, which woke scholars up to the fact that Biblical Greek was not some special Greek, but instead, it was the ordinary language of the common people, the man on the street. Thus, by comparing how the words had been used in these papyri, a clearer understanding of Biblical Greek emerged. As of the time of this writing, less than ten percent of these papyri have been published and studied. Most of the papyri were found in the top 10 feet 93 m] of the garbage heap because the other 20 feet [6 m] had been ruined by water from a nearby canal. If we look at it simply, this would mean that the 500 thousand documents found could have been two million in total. Then, we must ponder just how many documents must have come through Oxyrhynchus that were never discarded in the dumps. We have almost a half million papyrus documents (likely there were millions more that did not survive) in garbage dumps in the dry sands of Oxyrhynchus, Egypt.

The end result is that the New Testament has been preserved in over **5,836** complete or fragmented Greek manuscripts, as well as some **10,000** Latin manuscripts and **9,300 manuscripts** in various other ancient languages, which include Syriac, Slavic, Gothic, Ethiopic, Coptic and Armenian. Some of these are well over 2,000 years old.

The Hebrew Scriptures ended up in the hands of the Masoretes (Mas·o·retes \ ˈma-sə-ˌrētes) scribe-scholars ('preservers of tradition') who worked between the 6th and 10th centuries C.E., based primarily in early medieval Palestine in the cities of Tiberias and Jerusalem. The Masoretes have not been adequately appreciated for their accomplishments. These nameless scribes copied the Hebrew Old Testament Scriptures with meticulous and loving care. As for the early Christian copyists of the New

Testament, either literate or semi-professional copyist did **the vast majority** of the early papyri, with some being done by professionals.

It is true that the Jewish copyists, as well as the later Christian copyists, were not led along by the Holy Spirit and therefore their manuscripts were not inerrant, infallible. Errors (textual variants) crept into the manuscripts unintentionally and intentionally. However, the vast majority of the Hebrew Old Testament and Greek New Testament has not been infected with textual errors. For the portions impacted with textual errors, it is the many tens of thousands of copies that we have to help us to weed out the errors. How? Well, not every copyist made the same textual errors. Hence, by comparing the work of different copyists and different manuscripts, textual scholars, we can identify the textual variants (errors), remove those, which leaves us with the original content.

Yes, it would be the greatest discovery of all time if we found the actual original five books that were penned by Moses himself, Genesis through Deuteronomy. However, first, there would be no way of establishing that they were the originals. Second, truth be told, we do not need the originals. We do not need those original documents. What is so important about the documents? Nothing, it is the content on the original documents that we are after. And truly miraculously, we have more copies than needed to do just that. We do not need miraculous preservation because we have miraculous restoration. We now know beyond a reasonable doubt that the Hebrew Old Testament and the Greek New Testament critical texts are a 99% reflection of the content that was in those ancient original manuscripts.

Chapter 12 and 13 delves into the translation coming from Christian Publishing House.

CHAPTER 12 CPH Principles of Bible Translation for the Updated American Standard Version

The Old Testament was originally written in ancient Hebrew and Aramaic, while the New Testament was written in what is known as Koine Greek, namely, common Greek. The Bible has been translated into at least hundreds of other languages, possibly as many as 2,600. Of the billions of people who have read the Bible in the past and today, an extremely small percentage can read and understand the original languages and therefore, it must be translated into the common languages of the people. What principles should guide the Bible translation process, and how did these guide the rendering of the Updated American Standard Version? Generally speaking, there are two different translation philosophies: the **formal equivalence** and the **dynamic equivalent**.

Dynamic Equivalence is an interpretative Bible translation philosophy. Examples of such translations would be the CEV, TEV (GNT), NIV, NRSV, NLT, and so on. These translations committees take the literal translation and then alter it by going beyond what was written to give the reader what they believe the Bible author meant in place of the actual words.

Formal Equivalence is a literal translation philosophy, which means they seek to give the Bible readers what God said by way of his human authors. The meaning of a word is the responsibility of the interpreter (i.e., reader), not the translator. Examples of such translations would be the KJV, ASV, RSV, NASB, ESV, LEB, CSB, UASV.

Some who favor the dynamic equivalent translation philosophy have made claims that literal translations are strict, word-for-word, interlinear-style translations, asking the question 'would this enable the reader to get closest to what was written in the original languages?' This has become a pattern for those who favor a dynamic equivalent translation, to use an **interlinear Bible**, which is not a translation, to refer to it as a word for word translation, because they know that this phrase is tied to translations like the KJV, ASV, RSV, ESV, UASV, and NASB. Below is an example from Duvall and Hays in the third edition of *Grasping God's Word* (GGW).

Approaches to Translating God's Word

The process of translating is more complicated than it appears. Some people think that all you have to do when making a translation is to

> define each word and string together all the individual word meanings. This assumes that the source language (in this case, Greek or Hebrew) and the receptor language (such as English) are exactly alike. If life could only be so easy! In fact, no two languages are exactly alike. For example, look at a verse chosen at random—from the story of Jesus healing a demon-possessed boy (Matt. 17:18). The word-for-word English rendition is written below a transliteration of the Greek:
>
> *Kai epetimēsen autō ho Iēsous kai exēlthen ap autou to daimonion*
>
> And rebuked it the Jesus and came out from him the demon
>
> *kai etherapeuthē ho pais apo tēs hōras ekeinēs*
>
> and was healed the boy from the hour that
>
> Should we conclude that the English line is the most accurate translation of Matthew 17:18 because it attempts a literal rendering of the verse, keeping also the word order? Is a translation better if it tries to match each word in the source language with a corresponding word in a receptor language? Could you even read an entire Bible "translated" in this way?[128]

Because these authors favor the dynamic equivalent translation philosophy, they are not presenting the literal translation philosophy as it truly is. They give you, the reader, an interlinear rendering of Matthew 17:18, and then refer to it as a literal translation, which by association would include the ASV, RSV, NASB, ESV, and the UASV. Again, an interlinear is not a Bible translation; it is a Bible study tool for persons who do not read Hebrew or Greek. What is placed under the Greek is the lexical rendering, while not considering grammar and syntax, i.e., they are the words in isolation. Now, to demonstrate that the authors J. Scott Duvall and Daniel J. Hays are being disingenuous at best, let us look at the literal translations, to see if they read anything like the interlinear that Duvall and Hays used; or rather, do the literal translations consider grammar and syntax when they bring the Greek over into their English translations.[129]

---

[128] J. Scott Duvall and J. Daniel Hays, *Grasping God's Word: A Hands-on Approach to Reading, Interpreting, and Applying the Bible* (Grand Rapids, MI: Zondervan, 2005), 166.

[129] It should be noted that the Crossway Bibles' has names the English Standard Version (ESV) an Essentially Literal translation and the Holman Bible Publishers' has names the Christian Standard Bible (CSB) an Optimal Equivalence translation.

ASV	NASB	UASV
¹⁸ And Jesus rebuked him; and the demon went out of him: and the boy was cured from that hour.	¹⁸ And Jesus rebuked him, and the demon came out of him, and the boy was cured at once.	¹⁸ And Jesus rebuked him, and the demon came out of him and the boy was healed from that hour.
RSV	ESV	CSB
¹⁸ And Jesus rebuked him, and the demon came out of him, and the boy was cured instantly.	¹⁸ And Jesus rebuked the demon, and it came out of him, and the boy was healed instantly.	¹⁸ Then Jesus rebuked the demon, and it came out of him, and from that moment the boy was healed.

As can be clearly seen from the above four literal translations, the ASV, NASB, UASV, and the RSV and the essentially literal ESV and the optimally equivalent CSB, they are nothing like the interlinear that Duvall and Hays tried to offer us as a word-for-word translation, i.e., a literal translation.

Can the Original Language Text be Translated Perfectly into Any Modern-Day language?

There will most likely never be a perfect translation into any modern-day language. There are a few things that can get in the way of a perfect translation.

No modern language exactly reflects the original language vocabulary and grammar of Biblical Hebrew, Aramaic, and Greek. Therefore, at times, a literal translation of the Bible can be ambiguous or not fully convey the intended meaning of the original author. When we render an original language word into a modern language, it needs to be understood that we lose some sense of the meaning that would have been conveyed to the original audience in their language.

The same Hebrew or Greek word can have widely different meanings in different contexts. For example, the Hebrew word *zaqen* and the Greek word *presbuteros* can be translated "older man," or "elder," and both are sometimes used to refer to persons that are *advanced in age* (Gen. 18:11; Deut. 28:50; 1 Sam. 2:22; 1 Tim 5:1-2) or to the older of two persons (*older son*, Lu 15:25). However, it can also apply to those holding a position of authority and responsibility in the Christian congregation (*elders*, 1 Tim. 5:17), in the community or a nation. It is also used in reference to the ancestors of Israel (men of old, Heb. 11:2), as well as members of the Jewish Sanhedrin (*elders*, Matt. 16:21), and of the *twenty-four elders* (heavenly beings) seated on the twenty-four thrones around the throne of God (Rev. 4:4) Clearly, the context will determine what the author meant in his usage of these terms. The translator should always seek to reflect the literal rendering of the original language in every passage, but there will be some rare exception to this rule. Here are few of those exceptions.

Jesus' half-brother, James writes,

also the tongue fire the world of the unrighteousness the
6 καὶ ἡ γλῶσσα , **ὁ κόσμος τῆς ἀδικίας** ἡ
tongue is appointed in the members of us the one spotting up
γλῶσσα καθίσταται ἐν τοῖς μέλεσιν , ἡ **σπιλοῦσα**
whole the body and inflaming the wheel of the birth and
ὅλον τὸ σῶμα καὶ φλογίζουσα τὸν **τροχὸν τῆς γενέσεως** καὶ
being inflamed by the Gehenna.
φλογιζομένη ὑπὸ τῆς **γεέννης.**

James 3:6 Updated American Standard Version (UASV)

⁶ And the tongue is a fire, the world of unrighteousness; the tongue is set among our members, staining the whole body, setting on fire the course of life, and is set on fire by Gehenna.

We have several great examples of translation decisions within this one verse.

In rendering, "the world of unrighteousness," older translations and the 1995 NASB use the now dated term **iniquity**, which means "grossly immoral behavior." From the verb from which the participle James uses, "staining the whole body" we literally have **spotting the whole body**, somewhat ambiguous, so we should adopt the lexical rendering "stained," "defiled," or "corrupted." Then we have, "the course of life," which is literally **the wheel of birth** (existence, origin). Finally, translators of the Bible should avoid rendering the Hebrew Sheol and the Greek Hades and **Gehenna** by the word hell. By simply transliterating these words it will force the reader to dig deeper for the intended meaning of the author.

When dated terms are used (**iniquity**), they should be replaced with a corresponding English word (**unrighteousness**) of the original biblical text. The Bible translators can use such literal wording as (**stain, defile, corrupt**) in place of such ambiguous expressions as "**spotting the whole body**," which helps the modern reader avoid confusion. When the literal rendering comes across as making no sense (**the wheel of birth**), it is best to provide the sense of the original word(s). A translation of the Greek **geenna** is best transliterated as Gehenna. An explanation of what the translator is doing in the text should be placed in a footnote, giving the reader access to all of the information. Again, these are a rare exception to the rule that the translator should always seek to reflect the literal rendering of the original language in every passage.

Both the Hebrew Old Testament and the Greek New Testament render the original language words as "sleep" and "fall asleep," which refer to a sleeping body and a dead body. Below, we can see from the context of Matthew 28:13 that this is the physical sleep.

Matthew 28:13 (UASV)

κοιμωμένων koimōmenōn

Lexical: sleep; fall asleep

Literal Translation: asleep

Sense: to be or become asleep

Matthew 28:13 Updated American Standard Version

¹³ and said, "Say, 'His disciples came by night and stole him away while we were **asleep**.'

However, in the verses below the context is to be asleep in death; the figurative extension of the physical sleep in the sense of being at rest and peace; the person in the sleep of death exists in God's memory as they sleep in death; it is only temporary for those who are physically asleep so it will be true for those who are asleep in death.

Acts 7:60 (UASV)

ἐκοιμήθη ekoimēthē

Lexical: sleep; fall asleep

Literal Translation: asleep

Sense: to be asleep in death; the figurative extension of the physical sleep in the sense of being at rest and at peace; the person in the sleep of death exists in God's memory as they sleep in death; it is only temporary for those who are physically asleep so it will be true of those who are asleep in death.

Acts 7:60 Updated American Standard Version

⁶⁰ Then falling on his knees, he cried out with a loud voice, "Lord, do not hold this sin against them!" Having said this, he fell **asleep in death**.

1 Corinthians 7:39 (UASV)

κοιμηθῇ koimēthē

Lexical: sleep; fall asleep

Literal Translation: asleep

Sense: to be asleep in death; the figurative extension of the physical sleep in the sense of being at rest and at peace; the person in the sleep of death exists in God's memory as they sleep in death; it is only temporary for those who are physically asleep so it will be true of those who are asleep in death.

1 Corinthians 7:39 Updated American Standard Version

³⁹ A wife is bound to her husband as long as he lives. But if her husband falls **asleep in death**, she is free to be married to whom she wishes, only in the Lord.

1 Thessalonians 4:13 (UASV)

κοιμωμένων koimaōmenōn

Lexical: sleep; fall asleep

Literal Translation: asleep

Sense: to be asleep in death; the figurative extension of the physical sleep in the sense of being at rest and at peace; the person in the sleep of death exists in God's memory as they sleep in death; it is only temporary for those who are physically asleep so it will be true of those who are asleep in death.

1 Thessalonians 4:13 Updated American Standard Version

¹³ But we do not want you to be ignorant, brothers, about those who are **sleeping in death**, so that you will not grieve as do the rest who have no hope.

Here Paul is addressing the issue of those "who are sleeping" in death (*koimaōmenōn*). *Koimaō* is a common word for sleep that can be used as "to sleep," "sleep," or "fall asleep." However, it is also used Greek, Jewish,

Christian writings, and the apostle Paul's letters as a figurative extension of the physical sleep in the sense of being asleep in death. Paul is not using the common sense of the word here but rather he is using it to refer to the condition of the dead between death and the resurrection.

Psalm 13:3 (UASV)

פֶּן־אִישַׁן הַמָּוֶת: pen-išān

Lexical: lest I sleep the death

Literal Translation: lest I sleep in death

Sense: to be asleep in death; the figurative extension of the physical sleep in the sense of being at rest and at peace; the person in the sleep of death exists in God's memory as they sleep in death; it is only temporary for those who are physically asleep so it will be true of those who are asleep in death.

Psalm 13:3 Updated American Standard Version

³ Consider and answer me, Jehovah my God;
  give light to my eyes
lest I **sleep in death**,

1 Kings 2:10 (UASV)

שָׁכַב šāḵaḇ

Lexical: lie down; rest; sleep

Literal Translation: slept

Sense: to be asleep in death; the figurative extension of the physical sleep in the sense of being at rest and at peace; the person in the sleep of death exists in God's memory as they sleep in death; it is only temporary for those who are physically asleep so it will be true of those who are asleep in death.

1 Kings 2:10 Updated American Standard Version

¹⁰ Then David **slept in death** with his forefathers and was buried in the city of David.

Some have argued that the dynamic equivalent thought-for-thought translations (Then David **died** and was buried, NLT) are conveying the idea in a more clear and immediate way, but is this really the case? Retaining the literal rendering, the metaphorical use of the word sleep is best because of the similarities that exist between physical sleep and the sleep of death.

Without the literal rendering, this would be lost on the reader. Retaining the literal rendering, "slept," and adding the phrase "in death" completes the sense in the English text.

Nevertheless, there are times when the literal translation can be misunderstood or misinterpreted. **James 5:1** is translated, "But above all, my brothers, do not swear, either by heaven or by earth or by any other oath, but let **your "yes" be yes and your "no" be no**, so that you may not fall under judgment." The Greek is literally, "But above all, my brothers, do not swear, either by heaven or by earth or by any other oath, but let **yours is to be yes, yes, and no, no**, so that you may not fall under judgment." This would make little sense. Romans 12:1 is translated, "Do not be slothful in zeal, be fervent in spirit, serving the Lord." The Greek is literally, "Do not be slothful in zeal, be **in the spirit boiling**, serving the Lord." This would certainly cause confusion.

A literal translation is certainly more than a word for word rendering of the original language of Hebrew, Aramaic, and Greek. The corresponding English words need to be brought over according to English grammar and syntax but the translation at the same time must be faithful to the original word or as much as possible for the author may have use word order to emphasize or convey some meaning. In most cases, the translator is simply rendering the original-language word with the same corresponding English term each time it occurs. The translator has used his good judgment in order to select words in the English translation from the lexicon within the context of the original-language text. The translator remains faithful to this literal translation philosophy unless it has been determined that the rendering will be misunderstood or misinterpreted. The translator is not tasked with making the text easy to read but rather to make it as accurately faithful to the original as possible. The translator's primary purpose is to give the Bible readers what God said by way of his human authors, not what a translator thinks God meant in its place. The translator's primary goal is to be accurate and faithful to the original text. The meaning of a word is the responsibility of the interpreter (i.e., reader), not the translator. Nevertheless, extremes in the literal translation of the text just for the sake of being literal must be avoided.

Many modern-day English translations have taken the unjustifiable liberty in their choice of omitting the Father's personal name, Jehovah, from modern translations of the Old Testament even though that name is found in ancient Bible manuscripts. Many translations replace the personal name with a title, such as "LORD." The personal name of the Father is found thousands of times in the 1901 American Standard Version and will be retained here in the Updated American Standard Version.

UPDATED AMERICAN STANDARD VERSION (UASV)

OUR PURPOSE

Our primary purpose is to give the Bible readers what God said by way of his human authors, not what a translator thinks God meant in its place. – Truth Matters!

OUR GOAL

Our primary goal is to be accurate and faithful to the original text. The meaning of a word is the responsibility of the interpreter (i.e., reader), not the translator. – Translating Truth!

Why UASV?

The translation of God's Word from the original languages of Hebrew, Aramaic, and Greek is a task unlike any other and should never be taken lightly. It carries with it the heaviest responsibility: the translator renders God's thoughts into a modern language. The **Updated American Standard Version (UASV)** is a literal translation. What does that mean?

Removing the Outdated

- Passages with the Old English "thee's" and "thou's" etc. have been replaced with modern English.
- Many words and phrases that were extremely ambiguous or easily misunderstood since the 1901 ASV have been updated according to the best lexicons.
- Verses with difficult word order or vocabulary have been translated into correct English grammar and syntax, for easier reading. However, if the word order of the original conveyed meaning, it was kept.

More Accurate

- The last 110+ years has seen the discovering of far more manuscripts, especially the papyri, with many manuscripts dating within 100 years of the originals.
- While making more accurate translation choices, we have stayed true to the literal translation philosophy of the ASV, while other literal translations abandon the philosophy far too often.
- The translator seeks to render the Scriptures accurately, **without losing** what the Bible author penned by changing what the author

wrote, by distorting or embellishing through imposing what the translator believes the author meant into the original text.
- Accuracy in Bible translation is being faithful to what the original author wrote (the words that he used), **as opposed to going beyond** into the meaning, trying to determine what the author meant by his words. The latter is the reader's job.
- The translator uses the most reliable, accurate critical texts (e.g., WH, NA, UBS, BHS, as well as the original language texts, versions, and other sources that will help him to determine the original reading.

Why the Need for Updated Translations?

- New manuscript discoveries
- Changes in the language
- A better understanding of the original languages
- An improved insight into Bible translation

CHAPTER 13 The Updated American Standard Version (UASV)

Why UASV?

The translation of God's Word from the original languages of Hebrew, Aramaic, and Greek is a task unlike any other and should never be taken lightly. It carries with it the heaviest responsibility: the translator renders God's thoughts into a modern language. The Updated American Standard Version (UASV) is a literal translation. What does that mean?

It means that our primary purpose is to give the Bible readers what God said by way of his human authors, not what a translator thinks God meant in its place.

In other words, our primary goal is to be accurate and faithful to the original text. The meaning of a word is the responsibility of the interpreter (i.e., reader), not the translator.

Updated American Standard Version's Story

It has been a journey filled with many trials and tribulations.

An Idea is Born

In 1986, Edward D. Andrews became a Christian. However, he would fall away from the faith because he lost his faith to Bible critics. It would be in 1996 that he would find his way back. One night in the shower, he began to cry, to cry out to the Father. He pleads with the Father to show him the truth, to help him find the truth. The entire night was spent in prayer and tears. He had made a commitment that if God helped him get the books, he would study and study he did. He studied 6-8 hours a day, seven days a week for ten years. Not wanting to make the mistake that he did before, he studied apologetics, textual criticism, Bible translation process and philosophy, Hebrew, Greek, and many other subject matters, to the tune of over 3,000 books. He had become an apologist for the Bible, the faith and God himself.

In 2005, he decided to become an author. After being rejected by the big publishing houses, he decided to start his own. It was in 2005 that Christian Publishing House was in his mind. Shortly after that, he began publishing other books by Bible scholars. In 2007 he decided to get the official degrees that went with his self-taught education.

EDWARD D. ANDREWS (AS in Criminal Justice, BS in Religion, MA in Biblical Studies, and MDiv in Theology) is CEO and President of Christian Publishing House. He has authored eighty-two books, including THE TEXT OF THE NEW TESTAMENT, THE COMPLETE GUIDE TO BIBLE TRANSLATION and REASONABLE FAITH. Andrews is the Chief Translator of the Updated American Standard Version (UASV).

Edward D. Andrews is the founder of Christian Publishing House and the Updated American Standard Version. His vision began in 1996.

Trials and Tribulations

In 2008 the economy crashed, and the United States went into a great recession. Andrews had a small business that he was using for his family and funding Christian Publishing House and the Updated American Standard Version when in 2009 many of his clients cut back by removing his services. His business went under, he lost his wife, his house, his truck, and equipment, as well as being forced to move to an apartment. Soon, his finances would not even support the apartment, and he ended up homeless for two years. Through all of this, he continued to pen his books, get his degrees, and maintain his online publishing, as well as publishing other author's books.

He has continued in his fight for the faith, his battle for the Bible, and slowly he is building Christian Publishing House, translating the Updated American Standard Version, and Biblical Training Academy. You can support his translation work here: www.uasvbible.org/donation

OTHER BOOKS BY EDWARD D. ANDREWS

978-1-949586-92-3

978-1-945757-99-0

978-1-949586-91-6

978-0692728710

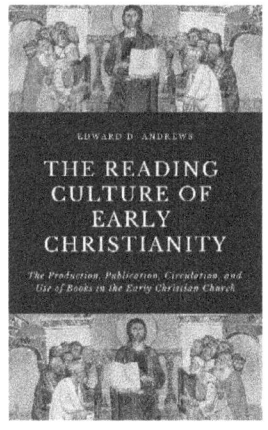

978-1-949586-84-8

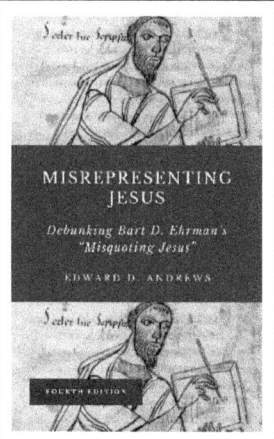

978-1-949586-95-4

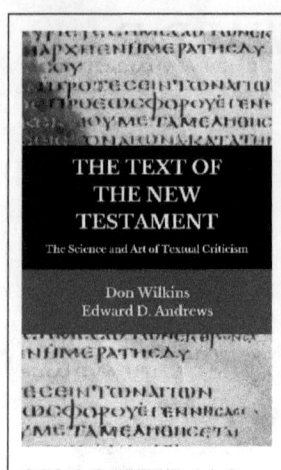

978-1-945757-44-0

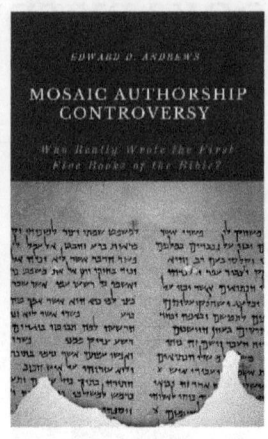

978-1-949586-79-4

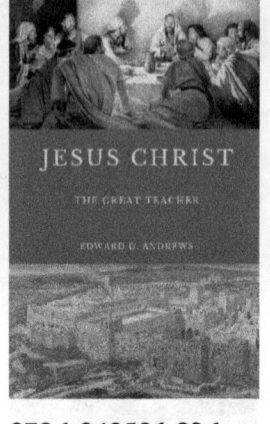

978-1-949586-83-1

Bibliography

Aland, Kurt and Barbara. 1987. *The Text of the New Testament.* Grand Rapids: Eerdmans.

Aland, Kurt, and Barbara Aland. 1995. *The Text of the New Testament.* Grand Rapids: Eerdmans.

Archer, Gleason L. 1994. *A Survey of Old Testament Introduction.* Chicago: Moody.

—. 1982. *Encyclopedia of Bible Difficulties.* Grand Rapids: Zondervan.

Arduini, Stefano, and Robert Hodgson Jr. 2004. *Similarities and Differences in Translation.* New York: American Bible Society.

Arndt, William, Frederick W. Danker, and Walter Bauer. 2000. *A Greek-English Lexicon of the New Testament and Other Early Christian Literature.* 3rd ed. . Chicago: University of Chicago Press.

Baer, Daniel. 2007. *The Unquenchable Fire.* Maitland, FL: Xulon Press.

Barnett, Paul. 2005. *The Birth of Christianity: The First Twenty Years (After Jesus, Vol. 1) .* Grand Rapids, MI: Wm. B. Eerdmans .

Barnwell, Katharine. 1975. *Bible Translation: An Introductory Course in Translation Principles.* Kenya: SIL International.

—. 1974. *Introduction to Semantics and Translation.* England: SIL.

Beekman, John, and John Callow. 1974. *Translating the Word of God.* Grand Rapids: Zondervan.

Bercot, David W. 1998. *A Dictionary of Early Christian Beliefs.* Peabody: Hendrickson.

Bock, Darrell L. 2006. *The Missing Gospels: Unerthing the Truth Behind Alternative Christianities.* Nashville, TN: Thomas Nelson.

Bock, Darrell L, and Daniel B Wallace. 2007. *Dethroning Jesus: Exposing Popular Culture's Quest to Unseat the Biblical Christ.* Nashville: Thomas Nelson.

Borgen, Peder. 1997. *Philo of Alexandria: An Exegete for His Time.* Leiden, Boston: Brill.

Brand, Chad, Charles Draper, and England Archie. 2003. *Holman Illustrated Bible Dictionary: Revised, Updated and Expanded.* Nashville, TN: Holman.

Bray, Gerald. 2010. *Translating the Bible: From William Tyndale to King James.* London: The Latimer Trust.

Bruce, F. F. 1981. *The New Testament Documents: Are they Reliable?* Downer Groves: Inter Varsity. Accessed April 03, 2009. http://www.libertyparkusafd.org/lp/Burgon/cd-roms/121bible.html.

Bruce, F. F., J. I. Packer, Philip Cmfort, and Carl F. H. Henry. 1992, 2003. *The Origin of the Bible.* Carol Steam, IL: Tyndale House.

Campbell, Gordon. 2010. *The Holy Bible: King James Version, Quatercentenary Edition.* Oxford, England, UK: Oxford University Press.

Comfort, Philip. 2005. *Encountering the Manuscripts: An Introduction to New Testament Paleography and Textual Criticism.* Nashville: Broadman & Holman.

—. 2005. *Encounterring the Manuscripts: An Introduction to New Testament Paleography and Textual Criticism.* Nashville: Broadman & Holman.

Comfort, Philip W. 2000. *Essential Guide to Bible Versions.* Wheaton: Tyndale House.

Comfort, Philip W. 2008. *New Testament Text and Translation Commentary.* Carol Stream: Tyndale House Publishers.

Comfort, Philip Wesley. 1992. *The Quest for the Original Text of the New Testament.* Eugene: Wipf and Stock.

Comfort, Philip, and David Barret. 2001. *The Text of the Earliest New Testament Greek Manuscripts.* Wheaton: Tyndale House Publishers.

Cruse, C. F. 1998. *Eusebius' Eccliatical History.* Peabody, MA: Hendrickson.

Dever, William G. 2001. *What Did the Biblical Writers Know, and When Did They Know It?* Grand Rapids: William B. Eerdmans Publishing Company.

Dewey, David. 2004. *A User's Guide to Bible Translation: Making the Most of Different Versions.* Downers Grove : InterVaristy Press.

Durant, Will & Ariel. 1950. *The Story of Civilization: Part IV—The Age of Faith.* New York, NY: Simon & Schuster.

Edwards, Tyron. 1908. *A Dictionary of Thoughts.* Detroit: F. B. Dickerson Company.

Ehrman, Bart D. 2005. *Misquoting Jesus: The Story Behind Who Changed the Bible and Why.* New York: Harper One.

Ehrman, Bart D. Holmes, Michael W. 1995. *The Text of the New Testament in Contemporary Research: Essays on the Status Quaestionis .* Grand Rapids, MI: Eerdmans.

Ehrman, Bart D. 2003. *Lost Christianities: The Battles for Scripture and the Faiths We Never Knew .* New York: Oxford University Press.

Elwell, Walter A. 2001. *Evangelical Dictionary of Theology (Second Edition).* Grand Rapids: Baker Academic.

Elwell, Walter A, and Philip Wesley Comfort. 2001. *Tyndale Bible Dictionary.* Wheaton, Ill: Tyndale House Publishers.

Evans, Craig A. 2002. *Fabricating Jesus: How Modern Scholars Distort the Gospels.* Downers Grove, IL: InterVaristy Press.

F. Garcia Martinez, Julio Barrera, Trebolle, Florentino Garcia Martinez, and J. Trebolle Barrera. 1995. *The People of the Dead Sea Scrolls: Their Writings, Beliefs and Practices.* Leiden: Brill Academic.

Ferguson, Everett. 2003. *Backgrounds of Early Christianity.* Grand Rapids, MI: Wm. B. Eerdmans.

Gamble, Henry Y. 1995. *Books and Readers in the Early Church: A History of Early Christian Texts.* New Haven: New Haven University Press.

Geisler, Norman L. 2007. *A Popular Survey of the New Testament.* Grand Rapids: Baker Books.

—. 2012. *Defending Inerrancy: Affirming the Accuracy of Scripture for a New Generation.* Grand Rapids, MI: Baker Books.

—. 1980. *Inerrancy.* Grand Rapids, MI: Zondervan.

Geisler, Norman L, and William E Nix. 1996. *A General Introduction to the Bible.* Chicago: Moody Press.

Geisler, Norman L. 1981. *Biblical Errancy: An Analysis of Its Philosophical Roots.* Eugene, OR: Wipf and Stock Publisher.

Geisler, Norman L., and Thomas Howe. 1992. *The Big Book of Bible Difficulties.* Grand Rapids: Baker Books.

Green, Joel B, Scot McKnight, and Howard Marshall. 1992. *Dictionary of Jesus and the Gospels.* Downers Grove, IL: InterVarsity Press.

Greenlee, J Harold. 1995. *Introduction to New Testament Textual Criticism.* Peabody: Hendrickson.

Greenslade, S. L. 1975. *The Cambridge History of the Bible, Vol. 3: The West from the Reformation to the Present Day.* Cambridge University Press: Cambridge.

Grudem, Wayne, Leland Ryken, John C Collins, Vern S Poythress, and Bruce Winter. 2005. *Translating Truth: The Case for Essentially Literal Bible Translation.* Wheaton: Crossway Books.

Hendriksen, William, and Simon J. Kistemaker. 1953–2001. *Exposition of I-II Thessalonians, vol. 3, New Testament Commentary.* Grand Rapids: Baker Book House.

Hill, Charles E., and Michael J. Kruger. 2012. *The Early Text of the New Testament.* Oxford: Oxford University Press.

Hoffman, Joel M. 2007. *AND GOD SAID: How Translations Conceal the Bible's Original Meaning.* New York, NY: Thomas Dunne Books.

Holmes, Michael W. 2007. *The Apostolic Fathers: Greek Texts and English Translations.* Grand Rapids: Baker Academics.

Hurtado, Larry W. 2006. *The Earliest Christian Artifacts: Manuscripts and Christian Origins.* Grand Rapids: Eerdmans.

James, M R. 1924, 2004. *The Apocryphal New Testament.* Berkeley, CA: Apocryphile Press.

Johnson, William A, and Holt N Parker. 2011. *Ancient Literacies: The Culture of Reading in Greece and Rome.* Oxford: Oxford University Press.

Jones, Timothy Paul. 2007. *Misquoting Truth: A Guide to the Fallacies of Bart Ehrman's Misquoting Jesus.* Downer Groves: InterVarsity Press.

Kaiser, Walter C, Peter H Davids, and Frederick Fyvie , Brauch, Manfred T Bruce. 1996. *Hard Sayings of the Bible.* Downer Groves, IL: Inter Varsity Press.

Keener, Craig S. 1993. *The IVP Bible Background Commentary: New Testament.* Downer Groves, IL: InterVarsity Press.

Kenyon, F. G. 2006. *The Palaeography of Greek Papyri.* Whitefish: Kessinger Publishing.

Kistemaker, Simon J, and William Hendriksen. 1953-2001. *New Testament Commentary: Exposition of the Acts of the Apostles* . Grand Rapids, MI: Baker Book House.

Komoszewski, J. Ed, James M. Sawyer, and Daniel Wallace. 2006. *Reinventing Jesus* . Grand Rapids, MI: Kregel Publications.

Lightfoot, Neil R. 1963, 1988, 2003. *How We Got the Bible.* Grand Rapids, MI: Baker Books.

Lindsell, Harold. 1976. *The Battle for the Bible.* Grand Rapids: Zondervan.

Linnemann. 1992. *Is There A Synoptic Problem? Rethinking the Literary Dependance of the First Three Gospels.* Grand Rapids, MI: Baker Book House.

Linnemann, Eta. 2001. *Biblical Criticism on Trial: How Scientific is "Scientific Theology"?* Grand Rapids: Kregel.

McDonald, Lee Martin. July 13, 2009. *Forgotten Scriptures: The Selection and Rejection of Early Religious Writings.* Louisville: Westminster John Knox Press .

Metzger, Bruce M. 1964, 1968, 1992. *The Text of the New Testament: Its Transmission, Corruption, and Transmission.* New York: Oxford University Press.

Metzger, Bruce M. 1994. *A Textual Commentary on the Greek New Testament.* New York: United Bible Society.

Metzger, Bruce M., and Bart D. Ehrman. 2005. *The Text of the New Testament: Its Transmission, Corruption, and Restoration (4th Edition).* New York: Oxford University Press.

—. 1964, 1968, 1992, 205. *The Text of the New Testament: Its Transmission, Corruption, and Transmission.* New York: Oxford University Press.

Metzger, Bruce. 2001. *The Bible in Translation: Ancient and English Versions.* Grand Rapids: Baker Academic.

Milligan, George. 2009. *The New Testament Documents, Their Origin and Early History* . New York, NY: General Books LLC.

Mounce, William D. 2006. *Mounce's Complete Expository Dictionary of Old & New Testament Words.* Grand Rapids, MI: Zondervan.

Munday, Jeremy. 2009. *Introducing Translation Studies: Theories and Applications (2bd Edition).* London: Routledge.

Oates, John F., Alan E. Samuel, and Bradford C. Welles. 1967. *Yale Papyri in the Beinecke Rare Book and Manuscript Library* . (New Haven: American Society of Papyrologists.

Orchard, Bernard. 1776-1976, 2005. *J. J. Griesbach: Synoptic and Text - Critical Studies* . Cambridge: Cambridge University Press.

Packer, J. I. 1965. *God Speaks to Man: Revelation and the Bible.* Atlanta: Westminster Press.

Pagels, Elaine. 1989. *The Gnostic Gospels.* New York: Vintage.

Parker, David C. 1997. *The living Text of the Gospels.* Cambridge: Cambridge University Press.

Porter, Stanley E, and Mark J Boda. 2009. *Translating the New Testament.* Grand Rapids, MI: Wm. B. Eerdmans.

Porter, Stanley E, and Richard S Hess. 2004. *Translating the Bible: Problems and Prospects.* New York, NY: T&T Clark International.

Poythress, Vern S. Grudem, Wayne A. 2004. *The TNIV and The Gender-Neutral Bible Controversy.* Nashville: Boardman & Holman.

Price, Randall. 2007. *Searching for the Original Bible.* Eugene: Harvest House.

Ray, Vernon. 1982. "The Formal vs Dynamic Equivalent Principle in New Testament Translation." *Restoration Quarterly 25* 46-56.

Rhodes, Ron. 2009. *The Complete Guid to Bible Translations.* Eugene, OR: Harvest House.

Richards, E. Randolph. 2004. *Paul And First-Century Letter Writing: Secretaries, Composition and Collection.* Downers Grove: InterVarsity Press.

Roberts, Alexander, and James Donaldson. 1994. *The Ante-Nicene Fathers.* Peabody: Hendrickson.

Roberts, C. H. 1970. *Books in the Graeco-Roman World and in the New Testament in the Cambridge History of the Bible, Vol. 1, From the Beginnings to Jerome* . Cambridge: Cambridge University Press.

Roberts, Colin H. 1979. *Manuscript, Society, and Belief in Early Christian Egypt.* London: Oxford University Press.

Roberts, Colin H., and Theodore C. Skeat. 1987. *The Birth of the Codex.* London: Oxford University Press.

Robertson, A. T. 1925. *An Introduction to the Textual Criticism of the New Testament.* London: Hodder & Stoughton.

Royse, James R. 2008. *Scribal Habits in Early Greek New Testament Papyri (New Testament Tools and Studies) (New Testament Tools, Studies and Documents).* Leiden & Boston: Brill Academic Pub.

Ryken, Leland. 2005. *Choosing a Bible: Understanding Bible Translation Differences.* Wheaton: Crossway Books.

—. 2002. *The Word of God in English.* Wheaton: Crossway Books.

—. 2009. *Understanding English Bible Translation: The Case for an Essentially Literal Approach.* Wheaton, IL: Crossway Books.

Schurer, Emil. 1890. *A HISTORY OF THE JEWISH PEOPLE IN THE TIME OF JESUS CHRIST (Volume II).* Edinburgh: T. & T. Clark.

Scorgie, Glen G, Mark L Strauss, and Stephen M Voth. 2003. *The Challenge of Bible Translation.* Grand Rapids: Zondervan.

Scott, Julius J. Jr. 1995. *Jewish Backgrounds of the New Testament.* Grand Rapids, MI: Baker Academic.

Souter, Alexander. 1913. *The Text and Canon of the New Testament.* New York: Charles Scribner's Sons.

Thomas, Robert L. 2000. *How to Choose a Bible Version.* Scotland: Christian Focus Publications.

—. 2002. *Three Views of the Origins of the Synoptic Gospels.* Grand Rapids, MI: Kregel.

Thomas, Robert L., and F. David Farnell. 1998. *THE JESUS CRISIS: The Inroads of Historical Criticism in Evagelical Scholarship.* Grand Rapids, MI: Kregel Publications.

Thompson, Edward Maunde. 1896. *Bible Illustrations.* Oxford; London:: Oxford University Press.

Torrey, Reuben Archer. 1907. *Difficulties in the Bible: Alleged Errors and Contradictions.* Chicago: Moody Press.

University, Stanford. 2012. *Calculating the Time and Cost of Paul's Missionary Journeys.* Accessed 07 12, 2014. http://www.openbible.info/blog/2012/07/calculating-the-time-and-cost-of-pauls-missionary-journeys/.

Vine, W E. 1996. *Vine's Expository Dictionary of Old and New Testament Words.* Nashville: Thomas Nelson.

Virkler, Henry A, and Karelynne Gerber Ayayo. 1981, 2007. *Hermeneutics: Principles and Processes of Biblical Interpretation.* Grand Rapids, MI: Baker Academic.

Wallace, Daniel B. 2008. *bible.org.* Winter. Accessed December 18, 2011. http://bible.org/article/number-textual-variants-evangelical-miscalculation.

—. 2011. *Revisiting the Corruption of the New Testament: Manuscript, Patristic, and Apocryphal Evidence.* Grand Rapids, MI: Kregel Publications.

Wallace, Daniel. 2011. *The Reliability of the New Testament: Bart Ehrman and Daniel Wallace in Dialogue.* Minneapolis, MN: Fortress Press.

Wallace, Robert Burns. 1929. *An Introduction to the Bible as Literature.* London, England, UK: Westminster Press.

Walton, John H., Victor H. Matthews, and Mark W Chavalas. 2000. *The IVP Bible Background Commentary: Old Testament.* Downers Grove: IVP Academic.

Wegner, Paul D. 2006. *A Student's Guide to Textual Criticism of the Bible: Its History Methods & Results.* Downers Grove: InterVarsity Press.

Westcott, B. F., and F. J. A. Hort. 1882. *The New Testament in the Original Greek, Vol. 2: Introduction, Appendix.* London: Macmillan and Co.

Westcott, B. F., and Hort F. J. A. 1882. *The New Testament in the Original Greek, Vol. 2: Introduction, Appendix.* London: Macmillan and Co.

Whiston, William. 1987. *The Works of Josephus.* Peabody, MA: Hendrickson.

www.ingramcontent.com/pod-product-compliance
Lightning Source LLC
Chambersburg PA
CBHW060155050426
42446CB00013B/2831